7 SECRETS OF SHIVA

Devdutt Pattanaik writes, illustrates and lectures on the relevance of mythology in modern times. He has, since 1996, written over forty books and seven hundred columns on how stories, symbols and rituals construct the subjective truth (myths) of ancient and modern cultures around the world. He consults corporations on leadership and governance, and TV channels on mythological serials. His TV shows include *Business Sutra* on CNBC-TV18 and *Devlok* on Epic TV. To know more, visit devdutt.com

7 SECRETS OF SHIVA

DEVDUTT PATTANAIK

First published by westland ltd in 2011

Published by Westland Books, a division of Nasadiya Technologies Private Limited, in 2022

No. 269/2B, First Floor, 'Irai Arul', Vimalraj Street, Nethaji Nagar, Alapakkam Main Road, Maduravoyal, Chennai 600095

ISBN: 9789395073080

10 9

Typeset by Special Effects Graphics Design Co., Mumbai

Printed at Thomson Press India Private Limited

I humbly and most respectfully dedicate this book to those hundreds of artists and artisans who made sacred art so easily accessible to the common man

Contents

Author's Note: On Context and Structure .... *ix*

1. Lingeshwara's Secret *1*

2. Bhairava's Secret *29*

3. Shankara's Secret *61*

4. Bholenath's Secret *95*

5. Ganesha's Secret *129*

6. Murugan's Secret *163*

7. Nataraja's Secret *193*

Acknowledgements *221*

Author's Note

On Context and Structure

Imagine a Western scholar. He, or she, is typically from Europe or America. All his life, he has been exposed to Judaism, Christianity or Islam, religions that frown upon any overt display of sexuality. To him, sexuality is almost always an act of rebellion, an expression of defiance against the establishment. It is seen as being modern.

So imagine his surprise when he comes to India and encounters temples embellished with images of men and women in erotic embrace. Imagine his bewilderment when he finds Hindus worshipping an image shaped like a phallus called Shiva-linga. This is what his ancestors, a hundred years ago, also encountered, and condemned as pre-modern, licentious and savage. The scholar finds them vicariously liberating. Keen to study and understand these images, he hunts for a suitable academy. He finds none in India. So he enrols in a Western institution, where he is guided by Western academicians and is expected to follow methodologies developed and approved in the West. He starts reading texts as he would read the Bible, not realising that texts do not serve the same purpose in Hinduism. He decodes scriptures and images using his own cultural frameworks as the template. His conclusions are published in respected academic papers that win him accolades from Western academia, but they discomfort, even horrify, the average Hindu devotee.

Most Hindus become defensive and, like their 19th-century ancestors, go out of their way to strip Hinduism of its sexual heritage. A few, especially those with political leanings, react violently, outraged by the conclusions. Accused of cultural insensitivity, Western scholars strike back saying that Hindus do not know their own heritage and are still viewing Hinduism through the archaic Victorian lens. Battle lines are drawn. They are still drawn. Who is right, the arrogant academician or the stubborn devotee? It is in this context that I write this book.

I have noticed that the divide between Western academicians and Hindu devotees exists in their relative attention to form and thought. Form is tangible and objective, thought is intangible and subjective. Western scholars have been spellbound by the sexual form but pay scant regard to the metaphysical thought. In other words, they prefer the literal to the symbolic. Hindu devotees, in contrast, are so focused on the metaphysical thought that they ignore, or simply deny, the sexual form. The Western preference for form over thought stems from their cultural preference for the objective over the subjective. Hindus, on the other hand, are very comfortable with the subjective, hence can easily overlook form and focus on thought. This book seeks to bridge this wide gap between academics and practice.

- The first chapter looks at the meaning of the Shiva-linga beyond the conventional titillation offered by a phallic symbol.

- The second chapter focuses on Shiva's violent disdain for territorial behaviour amongst humans.
- The third and fourth chapters deal with how the Goddess gets Shiva to engage with the world out of compassion.
- The next two chapters revolve around Shiva's two sons, Ganesha and Murugan, through whom he connects with the world.
- The final chapter presents Shiva as the wise teacher who expresses wisdom through dance.

This book seeks to make explicit patterns that are implicit in stories, symbols and rituals of Shiva, firm in the belief that:

Within infinite myths lies an eternal truth
Who knows it all?
Varuna has but a thousand eyes
Indra, a hundred
You and I, only two.

1. Lingeshwara's Secret

Imagination makes us human

Icicle Shiva-linga

Carved Shiva-linga

River stone Shiva-linga

Natural rock formation Shiva-linga

One day a sculptor was given a rock and asked to carve an image of God. He tried to imagine a form that would best encapsulate God. If he carved a plant, he would exclude animals and humans. If he carved an animal, he would exclude humans and plants. If he carved a human, he would exclude plants and animals. If he carved a male, he would exclude the female. If he carved a female, he would exclude all males. God, he believed, was the container of all forms. And the only way to create this container was by creating no form. Or maybe God is beyond all forms, but a form is needed to access even this idea. Overwhelmed by these thoughts, the sculptor left the stone as it was and bowed before it. This was the linga, the container of infinity, the form of the formless, the tangible that provokes insight into the intangible.

The name given to God was Shiva, which means the pure one, purified of all forms. Shiva means that which is transcendent. Shiva means God who cannot be contained by space or time, God who needs no form.

Shiva has been visualised as an icicle in a cave in Amarnath, Jammu; as a natural rock formation rising up from the earth, as in Buda Kedar at Tehri, Uttarakhand or Lingaraja, Bhubaneswar, Odisha; as a smooth oval stone from the river bed of Narmada placed in a metal trough as in Kashi-Vishwanath, Varanasi; or a sculpture of a smooth, cylindrical, free-standing pillar rising up from a leaf-shaped base, as in Brihadeshwara, Tanjore or the Chandramouleshwara temple at Unkal, Karnataka.

In the 12th century, in the land which is now called the state of Karnataka, lived a man called Basava, who encouraged everyone

Ishta-linga of the Lingayats

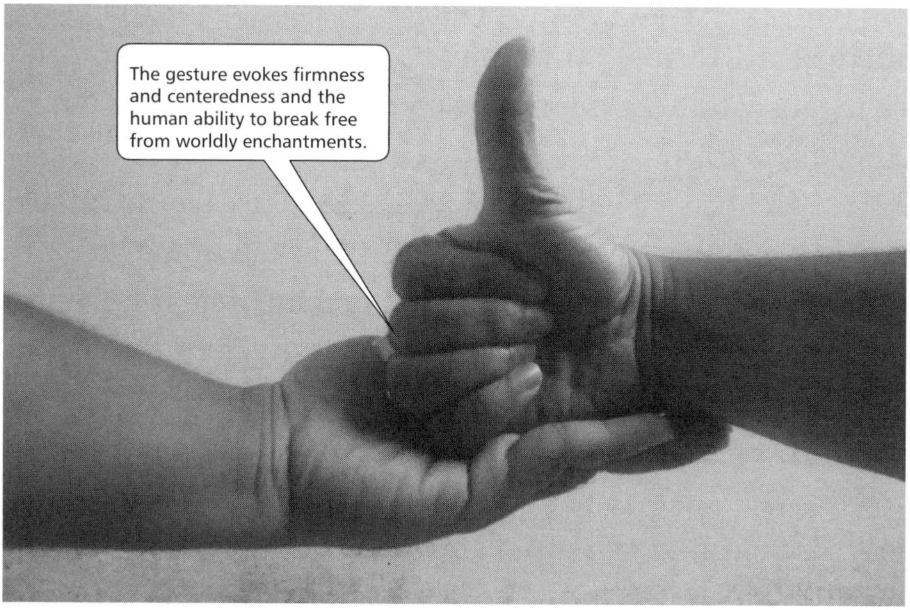

Hand gesture of a dancer showing Linga-mudra

to worship the formless, limitless divine in the form of a personal image, the ishta-linga, placed in an amulet and tied around the neck. The ishta-linga had no particular form and reminded Basava of the formless divine. He believed that by adoration of this idea through the formless form of the linga, humans would be able to break free from all divisions created by man on the basis of lineage, gender, profession or wealth. He inspired the Lingayat and Virashaiva movements.

Only humans can conceptualise the idea of infinity. Only humans can communicate such an abstract idea using various forms, such as words and symbols. This is because humans are blessed with imagination. It is the one thing that separates us humans from animals.

Humans can imagine because we have a highly developed brain, the cerebrum, with an especially large frontal lobe. This anatomical difference separates us from the rest of nature. So much so that in Samkhya, the Indian school of metaphysics, humanity or Purusha is seen as being separate from nature or Prakriti. This difference is seen as fundamental in the study of metaphysics. Because humans can imagine, the notion of a reality beyond the senses, a reality beyond nature, has come into being. Without the cerebrum there would be no imagination, and hence no notion of God!

In nature, all things have form. Each of these forms is limited by space and time. To sustain these forms one has to feed and one has to procreate. Eventually all forms are destroyed and replaced by new forms. Nature is thus a self-sustaining, predictable wheel of events where forms come and go. Only humans can imagine a

A stone Mukha-linga from Ellora

Brass masks that are placed over Shiva-lingas

world where all these rules are subverted: a world without forms, a world without limitations, a world without the need for action, or the obligation to experience a reaction, a transcendental world beyond feeding and procreating, creating and destroying, a still world, with no restlessness, only serenity, only bliss. In other words, humans can imagine a world beyond nature. This idea is contained in the linga.

In many temples of India, a head or multiple heads are carved on the linga stone, or a brass mask representing a head covers the linga-stone. This head is identified with Shiva. It is a reminder of the human head that is unique from all other heads in the animal kingdom. It houses the highly developed brain that can imagine and hence forge a path to the divine. This is the very same reason that sacred marks are placed on the forehead of devotees: to remind them of the critical role our brain, hence our imagination, plays in defining our humanity.

From imagination comes our vision of the world, our vision of our future, and most importantly our vision of ourselves, who we are and what we want to be. These visions may have nothing to do with the reality of the natural world around us. They may be improvements on what we remember or have been told. It is imagination that makes us realise that we are distinct from nature. In other words, imagination makes us self-aware. It is also imagination that makes us feel unique because no two humans can imagine the same thing. Imagination therefore makes us wonder about who we are, compelling us to analyse, synthesise, create and communicate. It is our imagination that will not allow us to stagnate. It propels us to improve. It propels us to grow.

Somnath
in Gujarat

Mallikarjun
in Andhra Pradesh

Mahakaleshwar
in Madhya Pradesh

Omkareshwar
in Madhya Pradesh

Vaidyanath
in Bihar

Bhimashankar
in Maharashtra

Rameshwaram
in Tamil Nadu

Nageshwar
in Maharashtra

Vishweshwar
in Uttar Pradesh

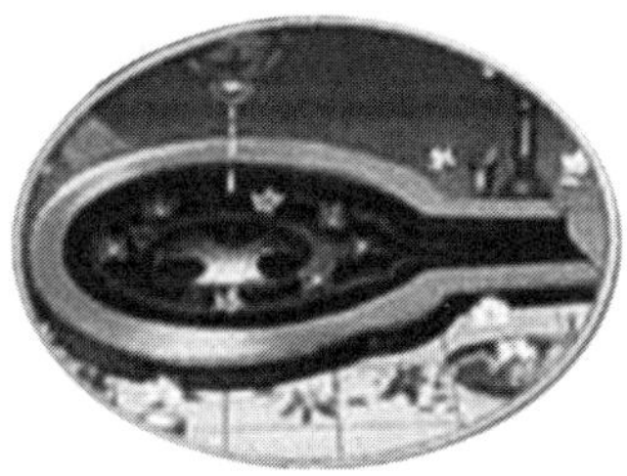

Trimbakeshwar
in Maharashtra

Kedarnath
in Uttarakhand

Ghushmeshwar
in Maharashtra

The twelve major Jyotir-lingas or self-illuminous, self-created lingas of India, mentioned in a hymn composed by Shankaracharya in the 8th century

In Sanskrit, the sound 'Brh' means to grow, to swell, to expand and enlarge. From this sound come two very critical ideas: brahman and Brahma. The former is a concept found in the Vedas and the latter is a character found in the Puranas. Vedas are the earliest sacred scriptures of Hinduism and are full of abstract hymns containing esoteric concepts. The Puranas were written later and use stories and characters to make those esoteric concepts more accessible. The Vedic brahman is a neuter noun, which means the vast, the boundless, and the infinite. Puranic Brahma is a proper noun referring to a form of God that is, very peculiarly and significantly, not worshipped.

The Hindu idea of God is rather complex. It cannot be explained without referring to Goddess. Most people, using the notion of God in the Bible as template, do not appreciate this and hence get confused. Goddess is nature and God is how nature is perceived by the human imagination. When the perception is incomplete and inaccurate, God is not worshipped, as in the case of Brahma. When the perception is complete and accurate, God is worshipped, as in the case of Shiva and Vishnu. In fact, when perception is complete and accurate, the divide between God and Goddess collapses. There is only one. That one is brahman. Brahma is God yearning for perfection that is the brahman. Hence the Vedic maxim, 'Aham Brahmasmi' which means both 'I am Brahma' – meaning 'I am finite', as well as 'I am brahman' – meaning 'I am infinite'. Every human being is in the process of moving from the finite to the infinite, from Brahma to brahman, on the path forged by the imagination.

Poster art showing three forms of God

The neuter brahman is also called the nirguna brahman or the formless divinity. To be worshipped it needs to become saguna, or possess a form. Brahma is God who creates all forms, hence is called the creator; but he has not yet found the perfect form and is still yearning and searching, making him unworthy of worship. Vishnu is God who has realised that no form is perfect and so works with the limited forms. This is why he is called the preserver and is worshipped in various forms. Shiva is God who breaks free from all forms, having found all of them limited, hence he is the destroyer who is worshipped as the linga.

Devotees need form to understand and seek the formless; through saguna is realised the nirguna. Hence they turn to stories, symbols and rituals of Shiva and Vishnu. Shiva is Hara, who is indifferent to form, while Vishnu is Hari, who is appreciative of form. In medieval times, there was much rivalry between devotees of Shiva and Vishnu as they showed preference for either Hara or Hari. Wisdom lies in breaking free from all differences, divisions and limitations so that infinity may be realised.

One day, Brahma and Vishnu were quarrelling. Brahma claimed, 'I created the world. I must be God.' Vishnu retorted, 'That you seek validation means you cannot be God.' 'Then who is God?' Brahma demanded to know.

In response, a pillar of fire appeared between them. It stretched up beyond the dome of the sky and down below the foundations of the earth. And the fire seemed to be burning without any fuel.

Both Brahma and Vishnu decided to look for the ends of this pillar of fire. Brahma took the form of a swan and flew up to

North Indian miniature showing Shiva emerging from a pillar of fire find its top. Vishnu took the form of a boar and dug his way down, determined to find its base. Brahma flew for months and years but there was no sign of the tip of the fiery pillar. Vishnu dug for months and years but there was no sign of the base of the fiery pillar. Finally, exhausted, the two returned to share their findings. 'This pillar of fire has no base,' admitted Vishnu. 'It is endless and infinite.' Brahma, however, lied. 'I found the tip. I even found Ketaki flowers on it. I have done what you could not do. I am greater than you. I must therefore be God.'

As soon as Brahma said this, the pillar of fire burst open and out came another god, who looked like a mendicant, smeared with ash and wrapped in animal skins. 'Liar,' he shouted pointing to Brahma. 'You lie so that you can delude the world and dominate everyone around you to feel powerful. You are not God.' He then turned to Vishnu and smiled. 'You admit the truth. You are humble enough to accept limitations. You are curious to know what lies beyond the horizon. You are not intimidated by uncertainty or afraid of ignorance. You are in the process of becoming God.'

Brahma trembled and bowed to this self-assured being. Vishnu watched him in awe. The mendicant identified himself, 'If the formless can be given a form then I am he. I am God, I am Shiva.'

Since that day the stone pillar or linga is worshipped by all, a reminder of the pillar of flames that appeared between Brahma and Vishnu. Those who look at this stone image as merely a stone image are like Brahma, people who lack imagination and who do not yearn for wisdom. Those who look at this stone image as a symbolic container of an idea are like Vishnu, people with imagination who yearn for the truth that exists beyond the tangible.

Stone carving of Lingo-bhava, the first appearance of Shiva

Temple wall sculpture showing Shiva as teacher

In nature, everything has a beginning and an end. In nature, fire needs fuel. The idea of a pillar without beginning or end, made of fire that needs no fuel, can exist only in the imagination and is hence worthy of representing reality that is transcendental, existing beyond the senses.

In order to communicate the idea of spiritual reality, one needs symbols. One depends on nature to provide these symbols. But all things in nature are bound by natural laws, hence inherently unsuitable to express the idea of spiritual reality. So one selects those symbols that are less fettered by natural laws, at least in perception.

The Pole Star, for example, is the only celestial body in the sky that does not move at all. It appears fixed. All the stars and the planets move around it. The Pole Star serves as the symbol of a world where nothing changes, nothing ages or dies. The direction marked by the Pole Star becomes the direction of aspiration, the direction of spiritual reality. In the north, lives Shiva, said the wise.

No one has seen the birth of a mountain or the death of a mountain. No one has seen a mountain move. Mountains thus represent the stability and stillness of spiritual reality. Shiva is imagined as living on a mountain. This mountain is located under the Pole Star, in the north. This mountain is called Kailasa. It is covered by snow, water that does not move.

Shiva is visualised seated under the banyan tree. Roots of this tree emerge from branches and anchor themselves in the ground and eventually become so thick that it becomes difficult to differentiate the trunk from the roots. One does not know where the tree starts and where the tree ends, like the limitless pillar of

Stone wall carving showing Lakulesh

fire. It also has an unusually long life, making it appear almost indestructible, defying the laws of nature. That makes it a symbol for Shiva.

Shiva, who emerged from the limitless pillar of fuel-less fire, is therefore visualised sitting under the Pole Star, on a snow-capped mountain, in the shade of a banyan tree. Through this form, the idea of spiritual reality is communicated.

The earliest followers of Shiva were mendicants who lived outside human settlements, in forests, and moved around with matted hair, smeared with ash, naked or dressed in animal hide, carrying cups made of gourds or skulls, and bearing a staff. These were hermits, people who chose not to be part of culture. These men were not interested in marriage or children or society or worldly life. They were interested only in realising the infinite.

The leader of these men was called Lakulesh, meaning the bearer of the staff, or lakula. It is not clear whether Lakulesh was the name of a man, or a title. Eventually, it became one of Shiva's many names.

The lakula referred to two things that are seen in Lakulesh images: either the staff or the erect manhood. Maybe it refers to both. Lakulesh images on ancient temple walls have faded over time. Typically he sports an erect penis, holds a staff in his hand and his eyes are shut.

Ancient Indian artists used the male body to represent the mind. This is because the male genitalia, unlike female genitalia, shows dramatic visual transformation between states of non-arousal and arousal. A flaccid penis indicates an unstirred mind. An erect penis

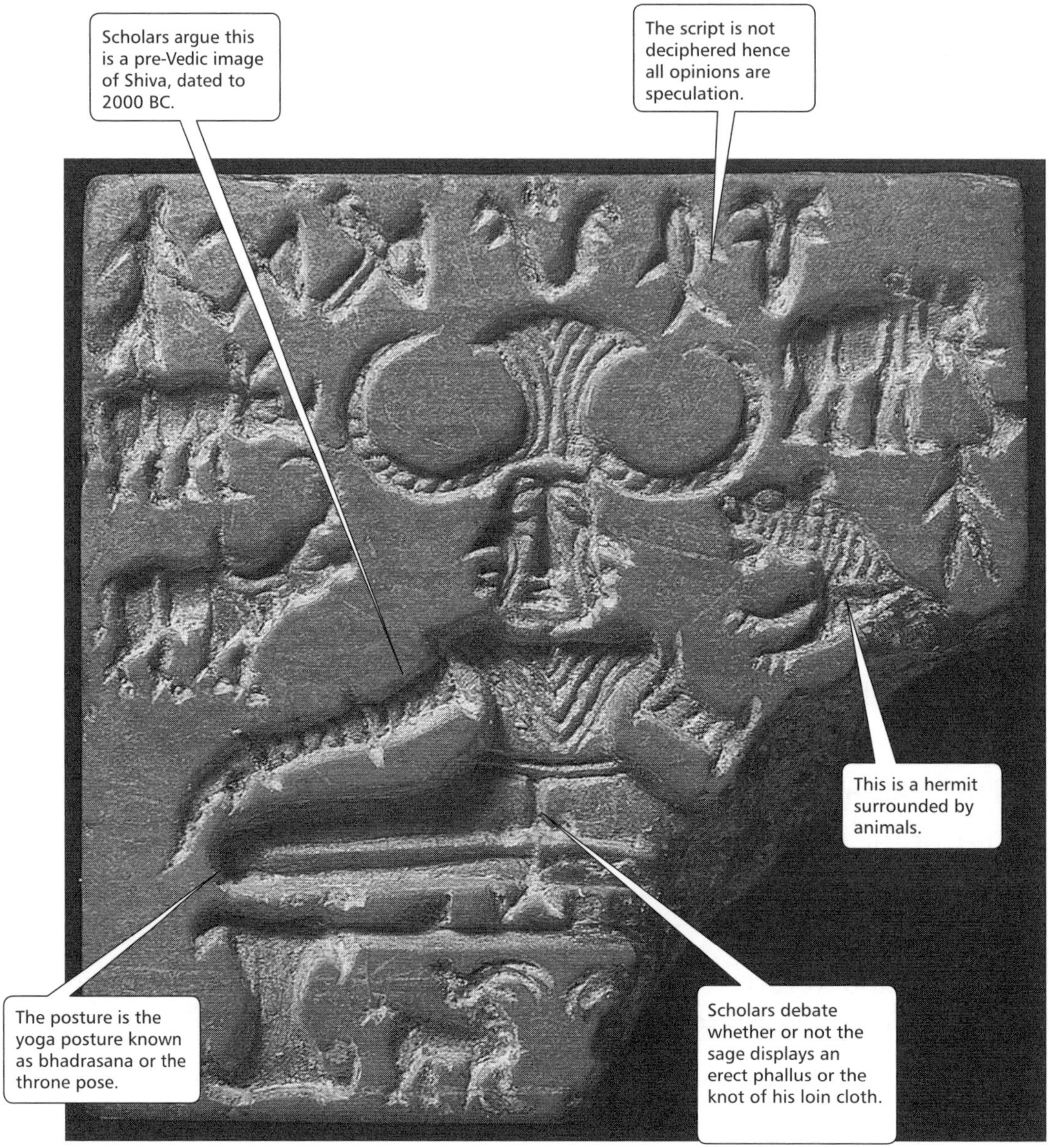

Indus valley seal showing a sage surrounded by animals

represents a stirred mind. The spurting of semen offers a very visual metaphor to show the submission of the mind to external stimulus. Eyes represent the senses. When the man's eyes are shut and his penis is flaccid, it indicates a mind that refuses to submit to external stimulus.

When the man's eyes are shut and his penis is erect, as in the case of Lakulesh, it indicates a mind that is stirred by an internal stimulus. Lakulesh's erection is not a product of sensations since he has blocked out all external stimuli. His bodily response is not dependent on a cause; it is causeless, it is not a reaction to something. That is why his aroused penis is considered self-created or self-stirred, swayambhu, hence worthy of adoration.

Through imagination one can experience everything from zero to infinity. Animals and plants do not have this ability; they depend on stimulations and memory. Humans have the power to block all stimulations that stir the mind and purge all memories that contaminate the mind, thereby experiencing imagination that is pure and pristine. This experience is the experience of pure consciousness. Realisation of this infinite power of the human imagination over nature's reality is expressed in the self-stirred erect phallus of Lakulesh.

Lakulesh's staff indicates the human ability to master the mind, stop it from responding to external stimuli, enabling it to cleanse the mind of all memories and prejudices. By doing this, the hermit outgrows dependence on things outside himself for happiness. Liberated from the confines of nature, he becomes master of his own contentment by discovering the infinite possibilities of imagination. Hence, the staff in his hand, symbol of power, authority and autonomy.

Poster art of Shiva

The self-stirred phallus of Lakulesh is a physical expression of an idea known as sat-chitta-ananda, which means tranquillity (ananda) that follows when the mind (chitta) discovers the truth of nature and of the human condition (sat) by purging itself of all memories and prejudice.

According to the alchemical principles of the body, a body's energy is utilised whenever the mind engages with the material world around it. To replenish these, we need food, water and breath constantly. As the body is used to generate more energy, it ages and eventually dies.

However, when the mind withdraws from material reality, it does not depend on nature anymore. It does not need to be fed. It generates heat autonomously without fuel. This is tapa, spiritual fire that does not need fuel, unlike agni that is material fire which needs fuel.

Tapa cleanses the mind, purges all memories and prejudices so that it experiences sat-chitta-ananda. It makes the body radiant, youthful and prevents it from aging. Tapasya is the process of lighting this fire. Lakulesh and his followers were Tapasvins, fire-churning ascetics.

Tapasvins hold Prakriti in disdain, because everything in nature is mortal. They seek immortality. In nature, everything is limited by space and time and restricted by form. The Tapasvin wants to break free from all limitations, expand into infinity, achieve what is called Siddha, the ability to acquire whatever he desires, not be fettered by gravity. And so the Tapasvin seeks to fly in the air and walk on water, expand and contract his size, change his shape. He

A traditionally decorated Shiva-linga without a mask

Shiva-linga with mask

seeks independence from nature. Withdrawing from nature is the first step in this process.

Detached from nature, a Tapasvin feels no pain, hears no sound, sees no image, tastes no flavour and smells no odour. In art, Tapasvins are shown as seated in cross-legged positions with creepers around their feet, termite hills over their bodies and serpents slithering around their necks. These men are intellectually, emotionally and physically liberated from all things material.

Tapasvins look inwards in their quest for independence and infinity. This inward gaze away from the material world is called nivritti marga, while the outward materialistic gaze is called pravritti marga. The inward gaze seeks the seed from where the tree comes; the outward gaze seeks the fruit of the tree. That is why Shiva is always bedecked with the seeds of the rudraksha tree. Rudraksha literally means 'the gaze of Shiva'. In contrast, Vishnu, patron of the outward gaze, is bedecked with leaves and flowers.

Shiva is the greatest Tapasvin. He spends no heat engaging with the outside world. All the heat he generates remains contained within his body. Naturally, the world around Shiva, unseen by him, gradually loses all heat and becomes cold. As a result, water stills and turns to snow. His mountain becomes Himalaya, the abode of snow.

The Tapasvin practises celibacy, refuses to have sex with women, and father children. Thus he destroys his family tree voluntarily. No other living creature can do this.

Plants are bound by nature to bear fruit and seed. Animals are bound by nature to mate. Humans are the only creatures for whom

Rudraksha tree

Fruits of the ruraksha

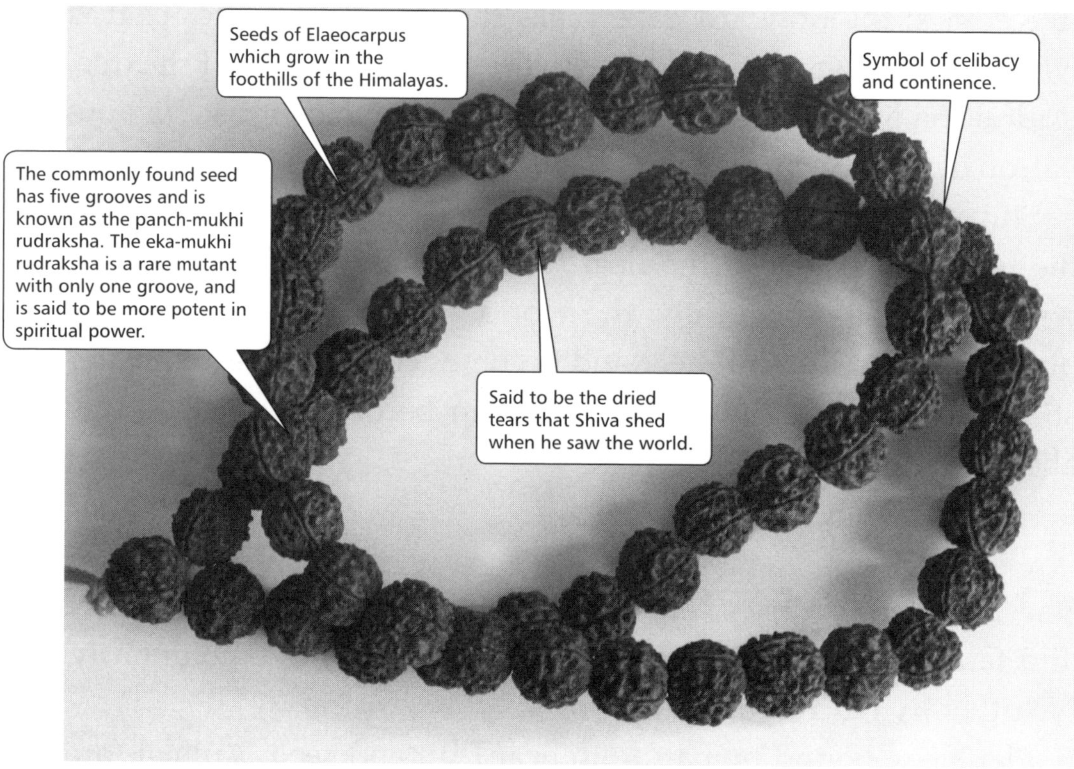

Rudraksha beads

reproduction is a choice. A male hermit represents the rejection of that choice; he cannot be forced to make a woman pregnant. Women can be hermits and also refuse to bear children, but they cannot be used to represent the idea of disengagement from the material world because the female body can be forced to bear a child. Artists used the male body to represent the voluntary mind and the female body to represent involuntary nature. If all males chose not to procreate, one can imagine the end of the human race. Humans are the only creatures who can voluntarily make themselves extinct, if the men choose not to act on desire. The male gender of Lakulesh is thus indicative of choice.

Shiva strings the seeds of the rudraksha around his neck, instead of sowing them under the ground. Thus he prevents germination. Thus the rudraksha-mala or chain of rudraksha beads represents celibacy.

In Tantrik physiology it is said that men have white seed (sperms in semen) and women have red seed (ovum in menstrual blood). The two seeds fuse to create a child. The followers of Shiva believed that so long as the flow of seed is downward, living creatures will remain mortal.

Plants and animals cannot control their urge to spill their seed. Women have no control over their red seed. Their menstrual cycle is fettered to nature's rhythms like the waxing and waning of the moon and the movement of the tides. Only the human male has the power to control the movement of his white seed. It can flow downwards in pleasure or to procreate — this results in mortality. It can be made to flow upwards with yoga. This generates wisdom, ignites the spiritual fire of Tapa and results in immortality. This upward movement of semen is described in Tantra as Urdhvaretas.

Miniature painting of woman worshipping Shiva-linga

Reverse movement of the semen is also a metaphor for the reversal of the senses so that they pay less attention to the material reality outside and more to the spiritual reality inside. This reverse movement is also known as the northern movement, towards the Pole Star, in contrast to the southern movement, out of the body, which results in children, family and social responsibilities. It is depicted in art as an erect phallus in a Tapasvin whose eyes are shut.

Shiva's holy city, Kashi, is located at a bend in the river Ganga where it turns and moves northwards instead of southwards. This reverse flow of the river is a reminder of what the human mind can do. Only the human mind, blessed with imagination, can challenge the laws of nature, withdraw from it and even break free from it. This is moksha, or liberation.

Shiva-linga then is at once the self-stirred phallus of the Tapasvin, the reverse flow of his semen, the burning of Tapa, the endless pillar of fire and the form of the formless divine. This is the Stanu, the still pillar of consciousness, the fountainhead of imagination, around which nature dances.

2. Bhairava's Secret

From fear comes all corruption

South Indian bronze showing deer in Shiva's hand

Bhaya means fear. And the greatest fear of all living creatures is death. Yama is the god of death. We fear him. We do not want to die. We want to survive.

To survive, we need food. But to get food we have to kill. Only by killing a living creature can food be generated. If the deer has to eat, the grass has to die; if the lion has to eat, the deer has to die. The act of killing and the act of feeding are thus two sides of the same coin. Death ends up sustaining life. This is the truth of nature. Shiva is called Kaal Bhairava because he removes the bhaya of kaal, which is time, the devourer of all living things.

Fear of death leads to two kinds of fears as it transforms all living creatures either into predator or prey. The fear of scarcity haunts the predator as it hunts for food; the fear of predation haunts the prey as it avoids being hunted. Nature has no favourites. Both the lion and the deer have to run in order to survive. The lion runs to catch its prey and the deer runs to escape its predator. The deer may be prey to the lion, but it is predator to the grass. Thus no one in nature is a mere victim. Without realising it every victim is a victimiser, and there is no escape from this cycle of life.

Fear of death creates the food chain comprising the eaters and the eaten. Fear of death is what makes animals migrate in search of pastures and hunting grounds. Fear of death establishes the law of the jungle that might is right. Fear of death is what makes animals establish pecking orders and territories. Fear of death makes animals respect and yearn for strength and cunning, for only then

The male head that is often placed over a Shiva-linga

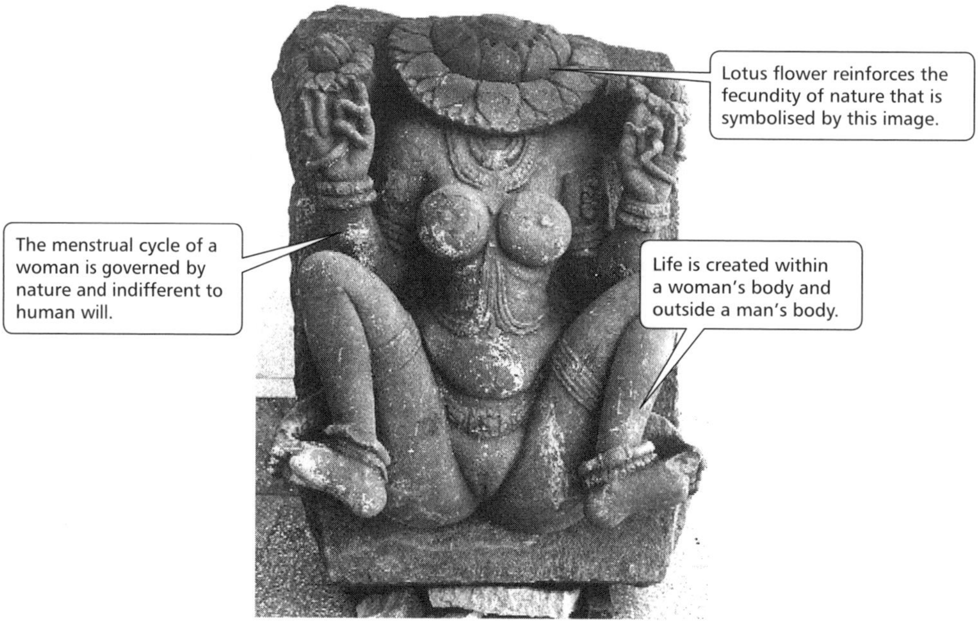

Stone carving of headless female body known as Lajja-gauri

can they survive.

Such behaviour based on fear is appropriate for the beast or pashu, but not humans. Humans have imagination and hence the wherewithal to break free from animal instincts. Humans need not be territorial or dominating in order to survive. Humans need not form packs or herds in order to survive. Humans can break free from the fear of death, shatter the mental modifications emerging from time. Humans need not be predator or prey, victim or victimiser. Shiva, who rises out of the endless pillar of fuel-less fire, shows the way.

Shiva reveals the power of the higher brain over the lower brain, the human brain over the animal brain. That is why he is called Pashu-pati, master of animal instincts. He offers the promise of a-bhaya, the world where there is no fear of scarcity or predator, in other words no fear of death. Shiva offers immortality.

Because humans have the ability to imagine, humans stand apart from the rest of nature. This division is the primal division described in the *Rig Veda*. On one side stands nature, the web of life, the chain of eaters and eaten. On the other stands the human being who can imagine a world where the laws of the jungle can be disregarded, overpowered or outgrown. Humans therefore experience two realities: the objective reality of nature and the subjective reality of their imagination. The former is Prakriti; the latter is Purusha.

Prakriti is nature who has no favourites. Purusha is humanity that invariably favours a few over the rest. In art, Prakriti is visualised as the female body without the head while Purusha is

Painting from Nepal of Bhairavi, the fierce mother goddess

visualised as the male head without the body.

The head is used to represent Purusha because the head houses the brain, which is the seat of imagination. The body without head then comes to represent Prakriti.

The body's gender is feminine because the head has no control over the natural menstrual rhythms of the female body; the arousal of the male body is, by contrast, influenced by the head.

The head's gender is masculine as indicated by the moustache because the male body can create life only outside itself within a female body, just as imagination can only express itself tangibly through nature.

Nature creates and destroys life without prejudice. Human imagination is the seat of prejudice. It has two choices: to imagine a world without fear or to imagine a world with amplified fears. When the Purusha outgrows fear and experiences bliss, it is Shiva, the destroyer of fear. When Purusha amplifies fear and gets trapped in delusions, it is Brahma, the creator of fear. Naturally, the former is considered worthy of worship, not the latter.

A childless couple were once offered a choice: a wise son who would live for sixteen years or a foolish son who would live till he was hundred. The Rishi chose the wise son. In his sixteenth year, Yama, the god of death, came to claim the son who had been named Markandeya by his parents. Yama found Markandeya worshipping a Shiva-linga. 'Let me finish my prayers and then I am ready to die,' said Markandeya. But death waits for no man or prayer. Yama hurled his noose and dispassionately started dragging the boy towards the land of the dead. The boy clung

Mysore painting showing Shiva overpowering Yama

to Shiva's linga and fought back. Yama refused to give up and yanked the boy forcefully. The tug-of-war between the boy and the god of death ended when Shiva emerged from his linga and kicked Yama away. Markandeya declared that Shiva is Yamantaka, he who destroys Yama. Markandeya became the immortal sage.

In this story, wisdom is intertwined with immortality. One becomes immortal when one outgrows the fear of death. Markandeya does at the age of sixteen when he clings to the Shiva-linga, which is the symbol of Purusha or spiritual reality. This is a metaphor for faith. Faith is not rational just as immortality is not natural. Immortality is an idea that appears in the human imagination in response to the fear of death. When one liberates oneself from the fear of death using faith, one becomes indifferent to death. Death then no longer controls us or frightens us. We are liberated. We achieve immortality.

Shiva's ash draws Markandeya's attention to immortality. Shiva smears himself with ash to remind all of the mortality of the body. When a man dies, his body can be destroyed by fire. What outlives the fire and the body is ash, which is indestructible. Ash is thus the symbol of the indestructible soul that occupies the body during life and outlives the body in death. The soul is atma.

Markandeya realises that only the fool derives identity from the temporary flesh; the wise look beyond at the permanent soul. Flesh is tangible but the soul is not. Flesh is fact but the soul demands faith. Atma defines all laws of nature — it has no form, it cannot be measured, it cannot be experienced using any of the five senses. It is a self-assured entity that does not seek acknowledgment or evidence. One has to believe it. There is no other way to access it.

Brahma has no faith. He refuses to look beyond the flesh. He

Poster art showing birth of Brahma

ignores atma, and so catalyses the creation of aham, the ego.

The ego is the product of imagination. It is how a human being sees himself or herself. It makes humans demand a special status in nature and culture. Nature does not care for this self-image of human beings. Culture, which is a man-made creation, attempts to accommodate it.

Brahma is every human being. He is described as emerging from a lotus. This is a metaphor for a child emerging out of the mother's womb. This is also a metaphor for the gradual unfolding of the imagination.

Birth is not a choice. And survival is a struggle, a violent struggle, plagued by fears of scarcity and predation. This is true for plants, animals and humans. But only humans can reflect on these fears and resent it and seek liberation from it.

Imagination makes Brahma think of scarcity in the midst of abundance, war in times of peace. Though he can rein in his fear, he ends up exaggerating fear. He assumes he has no choice in the matter. Like Markandeya, he can imagine Shiva, but unlike Markandeya he does not have faith in Shiva. He therefore does not discover atma, and finds himself alone and helpless before nature, a victim. Who is the cause of this misery, he wonders. Is nature the villain?

Who came first — the victim or the villain, nature or humanity, Prakriti or Brahma? Objectively speaking nature came first. Nature is the parent. Humanity is the child. Subjectively speaking, however, imagination caused the rupture between humanity and nature, imagination forced Purusha to visualise itself as distinct

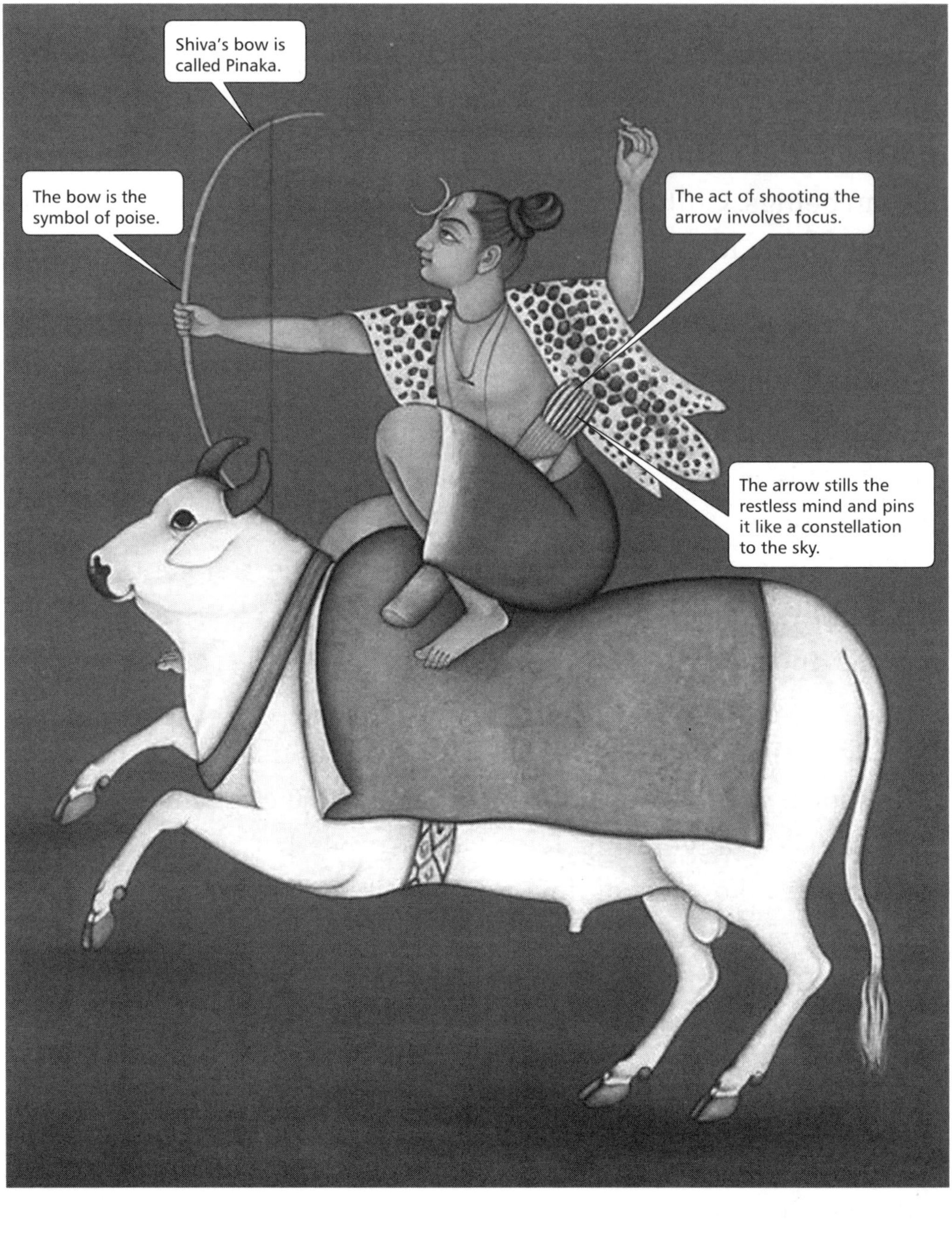

North Indian miniature painting showing Shiva as Pinaki, the bearer of the bow from Prakriti. That makes nature the child. Humanity then is the parent. Thus Prakriti is both parent and child of Brahma. He depends on her for his survival, but she is not dependable. She is the cruel mother and the disobedient daughter. He feels ignored and abandoned and helpless and anxious. He blames her for his misery. In fear, he allows his mind to be corrupted.

Brahma's expectations of Prakriti are imaginary. Nature does not love him or hate him. Nature has no favourites. All creatures are equal in Prakriti's gaze. Because Brahma can imagine, he imagines himself to be special and so expects to be treated differently by nature. This is because of the ego.

Brahma renames Prakriti as Shatarupa, she of myriad forms. Some forms nourish him and make him secure. Others frighten him. Brahma seeks to control nature, dominate and domesticate Shatarupa so that she always comforts him. Unlike the Tapasvin who sought liberation from nature, Brahma seeks to control nature.

The *Brihadaranyaka Upanishad* describes how Shatarupa runs taking the form of various animals and how Brahma pursues her taking the form of complementary male animals. When she runs as a goose, he pursues her as a gander. When she runs as a cow, he pursues her as a bull. He becomes the bull-elephant when she is the cow-elephant; he becomes the stallion when she is the mare; he becomes the buck when she becomes the doe. Shatarupa's transformations are natural and spontaneous. Brahma's, however, are the result of choice — he chooses to derive meaning from her, be dependent on her and in the process loses his own identity. The autonomy of his mind is thus lost, its purity corrupted, as it grows

Poster art showing a hooded serpent around Shiva's neck

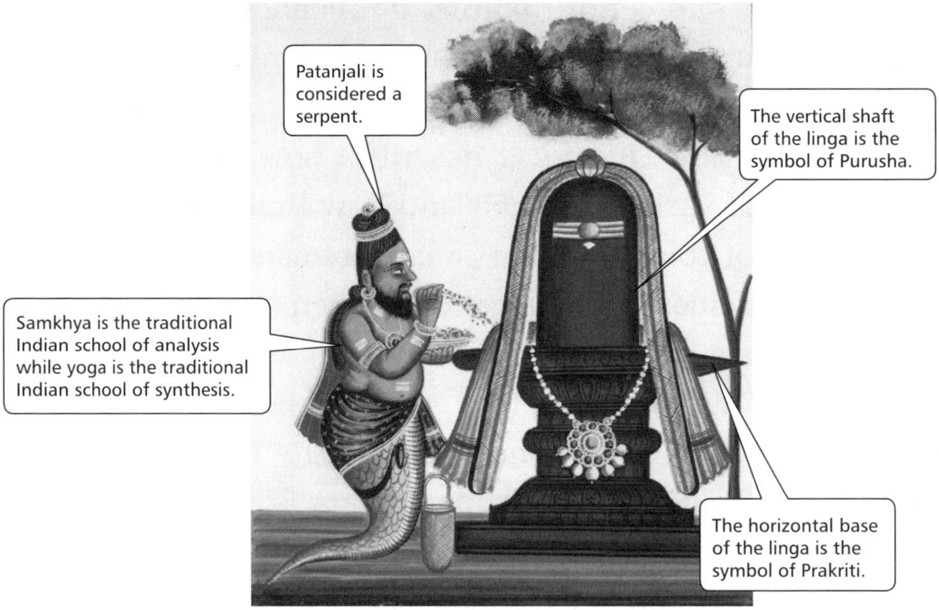

South Indian painting of Patanjali, the author of the Yoga-sutra attached to the world.

Brahma's chase of Shatarupa thus entraps him. It is the movement away from stillness and repose towards fear and restlessness, symbolically described as a southern movement, away from the still Pole Star. To stop him, Shiva takes the form of a bowman and raises his bow, the Pinaka, and shoots an arrow to pin Brahma to the sky. In other words, Shiva stills the mind.

The bow is the symbol of concentration and focus and balance, in other words, it is the symbol of yoga. Yoga is a set of practices that stills the restless mind. It is what can pin the deer down. The word yoga comes from the root yuj, meaning to align. Fear destroys the alignment of the mind; rather than accept the reality of nature, the mind seeks to change and control it. These attempts invariably fail, creating frustration and fear and confusion that blinds one to spiritual reality. Yoga restores mental alignment so that nature is seen for what it is. Witnessing Prakriti will provoke the journey towards Purusha. Rather than blaming nature or clinging to the flesh, one will find refuge in atma. Shiva is therefore called Yogeshwara, lord of yoga.

Seated coiled around Shiva's neck is the hooded cobra. The cobra is unique amongst all serpents as it possesses a hood that it spreads whenever it is still. The hooded cobra around Shiva's neck thus represents stillness which contrasts with the restlessness of nature. Shiva pins Brahma down so that he stops and observes nature's dance, and aligns himself with her rhythms rather than manipulating them to suit his whims.

It is said that the serpent around Shiva's neck is Patanjali who wrote the Yoga-sutra, the aphorisms of yoga. In it, he defines yoga as the unbinding of the knots of the imagination. Brahma creates

Poster art of Batuk Bhairava

these knots as he pursues Shatarupa; Shiva destroys them.

In the *Linga Purana*, Shiva howls when he witnesses Brahma chasing Shatarupa. It is a howl of despair and disgust. He mourns the corruption of the mind. Shiva, the howler, is called Rudra.

Rudra watches as Brahma sprouts four heads facing the four directions as he seeks to gaze upon Prakriti at all times in his attempt to control her. Brahma then sprouts a fifth head on top of the first four. This sprouting of heads refers to the gradual contamination of the mind, its knotting and crumpling with fear and insecurity as the desire to dominate and control takes over.

The first four face the reality of nature in every direction; the fifth simply ignores the reality of nature. It is the head of delusion. It is called aham, Brahma's imagination of himself, his self-image or ego. The fifth head of Brahma declares Brahma as the lord and master of Prakriti. This claim over nature is humanity's greatest delusion.

Hoping to shatter this delusion, Shiva uses his sharp nail and wrenches off the fifth head of Brahma. He becomes Kapalika, the skull bearer. Shiva severs the head that deludes Brahma into believing he created objective reality or Prakriti, when in fact he has only created his own subjective reality, the Brahmanda.

Prakriti is nature. Brahmanda is culture. Prakriti creates man. Man creates Brahmanda. Prakriti is objective reality. Brahmanda is subjective reality. Atma witnesses Prakriti, aham constructs Brahmanda.

Kala Bhairava images from temple walls of north India

Every human being has his own cerebrum, hence is subject to his own imagination of his self and the world around him, which is why every human being imagines himself to be special. Every human being is thus Brahma, creator of his own Brahmanda. Prakriti is common to all living creatures but Brahmanda is unique to a Brahma. As many Brahmas, as many imaginations, as many Brahmandas.

Prakriti is the universal mother of all Brahmas. Brahmanda is, however, daughter of the particular Brahma who creates her. Nature does not consider any Brahma special. Every Brahma believes he is special in his own self-constructed subjective reality.

Every human being compares his subjective reality with nature and finds nature inadequate. This dissatisfaction provides an opportunity to outgrow dependence on nature, hence fear. But instead of looking inwards, Brahma looks outwards. Rather than take control of his mind, he chooses to take control of nature. He proceeds to domesticate the world around him. Every Brahma creates Brahmanda for his own pleasure or bhoga, indifferent to the impact it has on others. This self-indulgent act is described in narratives as Brahma pursuing his own daughter. By equating it with incest, a taboo in human society, the scriptures express their disdain for the pursuit of aham over atma, bhoga over yoga.

The story of Brahma chasing his daughter is taken literally to explain why Brahma is not worshipped. Metaphorically, it refers to the inappropriate relationship of humanity and nature. Rather than pursuing atma and becoming independent of nature, man chooses to pursue aham and dominate nature. This does not allay fear, it only amplifies fear.

Shiva mocks Brahma's delusion by always appearing in a state

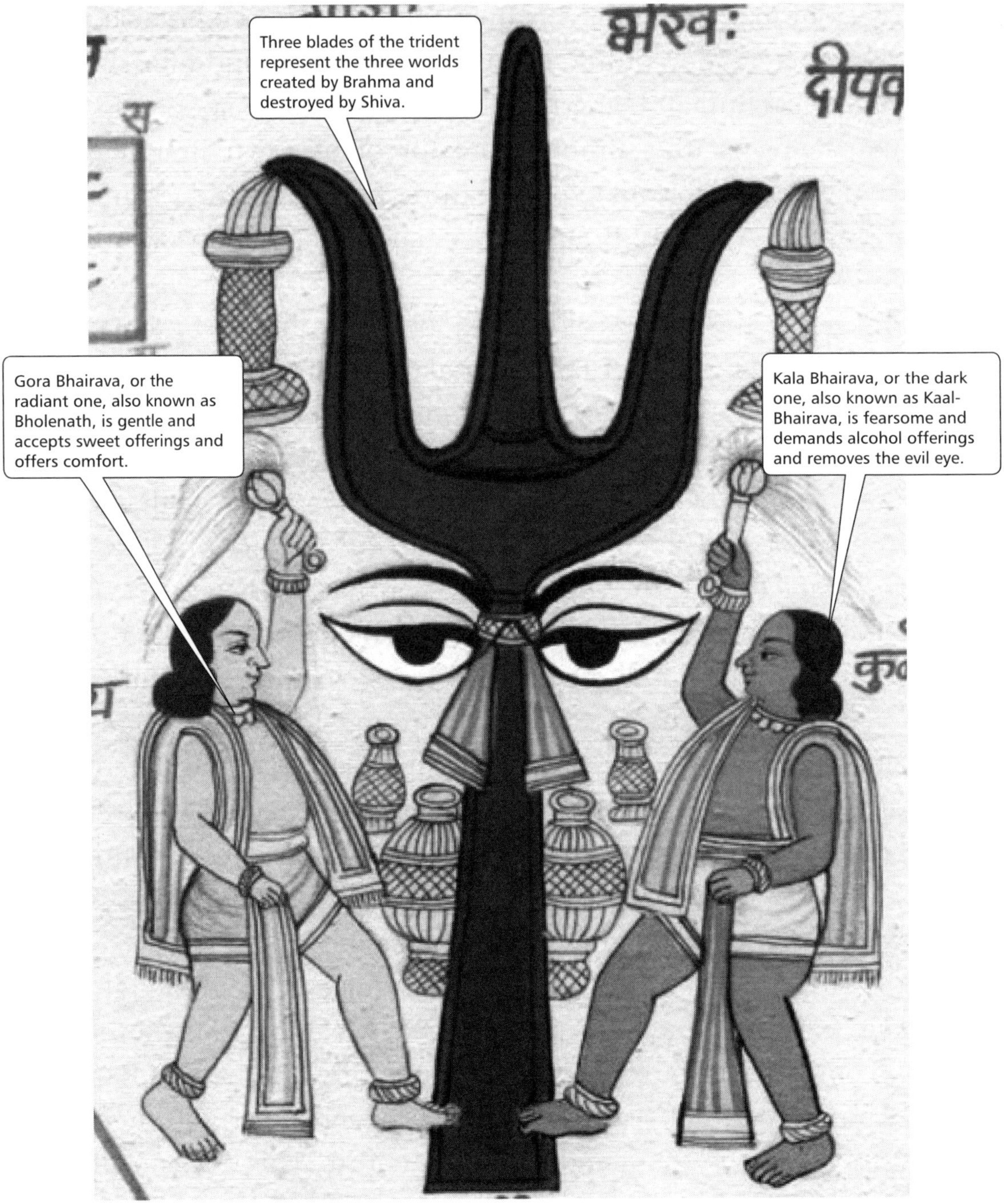

Tantrik miniature painting of Gora Bhairava and Kala Bhairava of intoxication. He is always shown drinking or smoking narcotic hemp. In intoxication, one refuses to accept reality and assumes oneself to be the master of the world. When the reference point is aham, not atma, when the world is only Brahmanda not Prakriti, one is as deluded as one who is intoxicated.

Brahmanda creates artificial value. In Brahmanda, we are either heroes or victims who matter. In Prakriti, however, we are just another species of animal who need nourishment and security and who will eventually die.

Realisation of this truth creates angst. Brahma wonders what is the point of existence then. He finds no answer and a sense of invalidation creeps in. It makes him restless and anxious. A life with imagination but no meaning is frightening. The human mind cannot accept this and so goes into denial. It seeks activities that fill the empty void created by time. It seeks to occupy the mind with meaningless activity so that it is distracted from facing the emptiness of existence. That is why human beings get obsessed with games and recreational activities that enable time to pass.

Shiva recognises this and so holds a damaru in his hand. A damaru is a rattle-drum that is used to distract and train a monkey. The monkey here represents the mind which is restless and angst-ridden. Unable to find meaning, it yearns to be occupied. Shiva rattles the drum to comfort Brahma's mind. He hopes that, eventually, Brahma will realise that meaning will only come by moving towards atma rather than aham, pursuing yoga instead of bhoga, choosing Prakriti not Brahmanda.

Recurring theme of three visible in poster images of Shiva

But Brahma stubbornly refuses to take the journey towards Purusha. He is determined to find identity and meaning through Prakriti alone. Brahma divides subjective reality into two parts: what belongs to him and what does not belong to him. Property is thus created. It is humankind's greatest delusion through which humanity seeks to generate meaning and identity.

Animals have territory but humans create property. Territory is held on to by brute force and cunning; it cannot be inherited; it enables animals to survive. Property, on the other hand, is created by man-made rules; take away the rules and there is no property. Rules also govern relationships in culture, creating families to whom property can be bequeathed. Neither wealth nor family is a natural phenomenon, both are cultural constructions, hence need to be codified and enforced through courts.

Through the idea of property, Brahma hopes to outsmart Yama. A human being can die, but his property and his family can outlive him.

Brahma splits Brahmanda into three parts: me, mine and what is not mine. This is Tripura, the three worlds. Each of these three worlds is mortal. The 'me' is made up of the mind and body. 'Mine' is made up of property, knowledge, family and status. 'Not mine' is made up of all the other things that exist in the world over which one has no authority. Even animals have a 'me' but only humans have 'mine' and 'not mine'. Human self-image is thus expanded beyond the body and includes possessions.

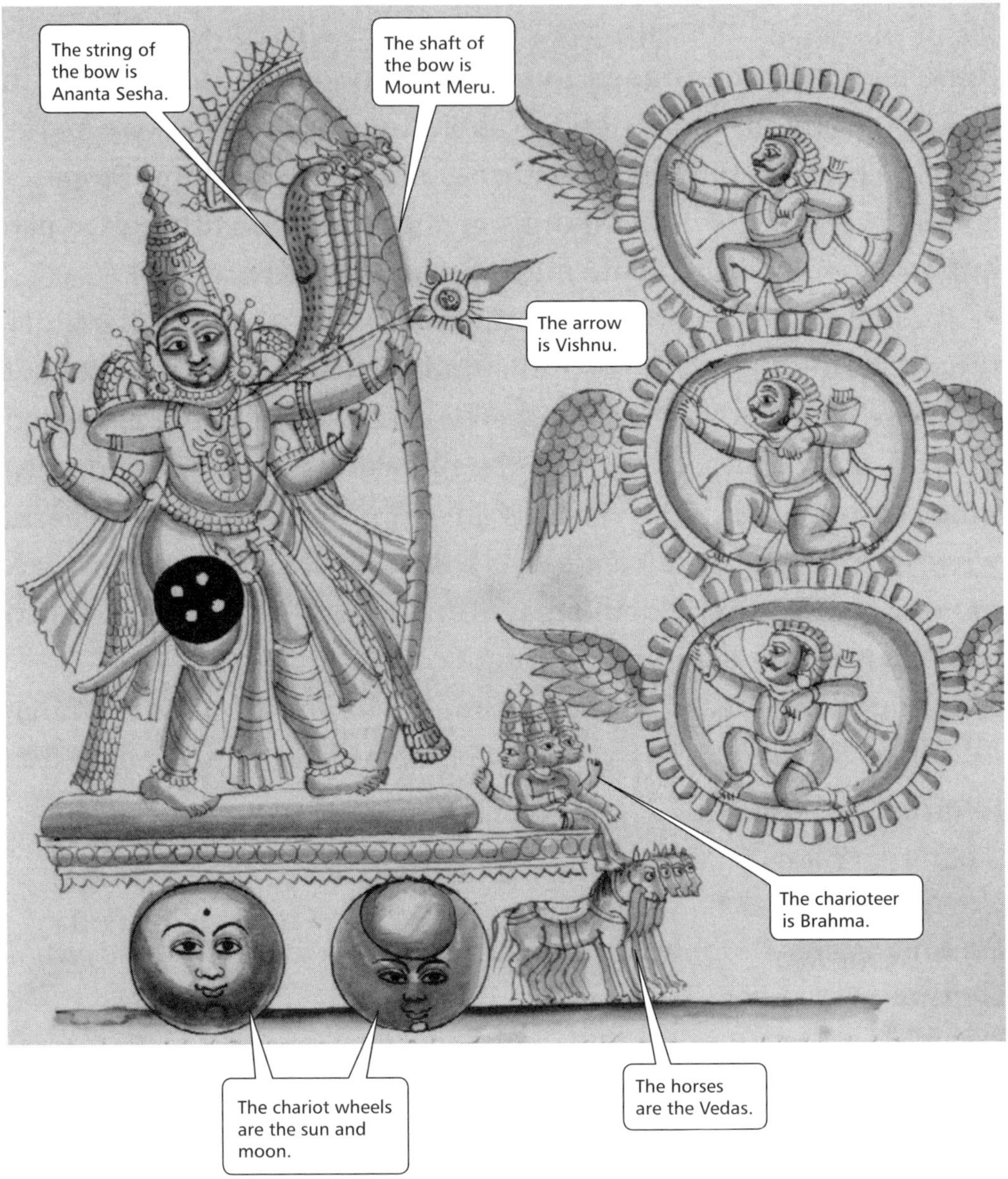

South Indian painting of Shiva as Tripurantaka, destroying three cities

Humans identify themselves with other things beside their body, hence get hurt when those things get attacked. A man derives his self-worth from his looks and his car. When his looks go, or his car gets damaged, his tranquillity is lost. Tranquillity is also lost when he yearns for things that are not his, things that belong to others. Anxiety and restlessness thus have roots in the notions of 'mine' and 'not mine', which depend on imagination for their survival.

At every Hindu ritual, 'Shanti, shanti, shanti,' is chanted. This means peace thrice over. Humans yearn to come to terms with the three worlds. This can only happen when we recognise the true nature of the three worlds we have created. Realisation of the true nature of Tripura will unfortunately reveal their mortal nature and the futility of clinging to it. Shiva is Tripurantaka, who reveals this reality and hence destroys Tripura.

The story goes that three demons created three flying cities and spread havoc in the cosmos. So the gods called upon Shiva to destroy these cities. The cities could be destroyed only with a single arrow. And so one had to wait for the right moment when the three cities were perfectly aligned in a straight line. Shiva decided to chase the three cities until this moment arrived.

The earth was Shiva's chariot; the sun and moon were its wheels; the four Vedas were its horses; Brahma himself was the charioteer. Mount Meru, axis of space, was the shaft of Shiva's bow while Sesha, the serpent of time, was the string. Vishnu was the arrow.

Shiva chased the three cities and waited for the moment when they were all aligned. At that moment, he released the arrow and destroyed all three cities in an instant. He collected the ashes of these cities and smeared them across his forehead as three parallel lines. This was the Tripundra, the sacred mark of Shiva. It

The fearsome Bhairava who protects Nepal

Kaal Bhairava of Varanasi

communicated to the world that the body, the property and the rest of nature, the three worlds created by Brahma, are mortal. When they are destroyed, what remains is Purusha, the soul.

The lines are drawn horizontally. In mythic art, vertical lines associated with Vishnu represent activity, while horizontal lines represent inertia. Shiva's mark is horizontal to remind us that nothing needs to be done actively to destroy the three worlds. Eventually, inevitably, the body will die, the property will go and the divide between 'mine' and 'not mine' will collapse as Prakriti stakes her claim. Shiva has infinite patience, which is why he is able to wait for the moment when the three cities align themselves, ready to be struck down by his arrow.

The number three plays a key role in Shiva's mythology. His sacred mark is composed of three parallel lines. He holds in his hand a trident, a weapon with three blades. He is offered in temples the sacred bilva leaf which is a sprig with three leaves. Shiva holds the shaft of the trident just as the devotee holds the stem of the bilva sprig. What is held is the immortal soul; the three blades and the three leaves represent the three worlds that Brahma creates and values, which need to be given up if one seeks, 'Shanti, shanti, shanti.'

Bhairava or Hara, the remover of fear, is visualised as a child riding a dog and holding a human head in his hand. The childlike form of Bhairava is to draw attention to his innocence and purity. There is no guile behind his actions. The head that he holds in his hand is the fifth head of Brahma, which is full of amplified fear and has no faith. This fifth head constructs the self-image. This fifth head

Southeast-Asian image of Bhairava

constructs Tripura, which Shiva destroys. The dog that Bhairava rides represents the human mind and how it regresses to animal nature when governed by fear.

Symbolically speaking, dogs are considered inauspicious in Hinduism. Dogs are most attached to their masters: wagging their tail when they get approval and attention, and whining when they do not. This makes the dog the symbol of the ego. Like the dog, aham blooms when praised and given attention, and it withers when ignored. Ego or ahamkara has no independent existence of its own but is constructed by Brahma and dependent on Brahmanda in an attempt to outgrow fear. It ends up amplifying fear.

Dogs also remind us of the notion of territory. Dogs spray urine to mark their territory; even when they are domesticated and provided for, they mark territory, indicating their lack of faith. They bark and bite to defend their territory. They fight over bones with other dogs. While dogs do it for their survival, humans behave similarly as they fight over their property and defend their rights. Humans seek the survival not of their bodies, as in the case of animals, but of their self-image, which is a combination of body and property. Property includes not just wealth, but also family and status. Without property there is no meaning, without meaning there is only fear.

Bhairava rides the dog to remind us of our animal instincts and our amplified fears that have constructed the notion of property. Like dogs we cling to 'me' and 'mine' and are wary of what is 'not mine'. We call this love, but it is in fact attachment, as they give us identity and meaning. Bhairava invites us to break this attachment, cut the fifth head of Brahma, cleanse the mind of all corruption, and discover the world where there is genuine freedom from fear.

Poster art of Datta, the gentle form of Bhairava

Many followers of Shiva worship Bhairava in a gentler form, as Datta, the three-headed sage who has four dogs around him and a cow behind him. Datta is called Adi-nath, the primal teacher of all mendicants.

Datta's three heads represent Brahma, Vishnu and Shiva, who constantly create, sustain and destroy. The future is created, the present is sustained and the past is destroyed. Datta does not cling to any construction. He does not fear any destruction.

His four dogs are a reminder of our fears. The cow reminds us of our faith. The cow walks behind Datta; he does not turn around to check if she is following him. He knows she is. The dogs are our fears walking in front of Datta, constantly turning back to see if he is behind them. They do not have faith. They constantly need reassurance.

Datta wanders freely without a care in the world. Nothing fetters him. No property binds him. Having achieved the full potential of his human brain, he has outgrown fear. He trusts nature. Prakriti, visualised as the headless female body, who is Bhairavi, for the frightened Brahma, ends up as his companion, his friend, his mother, sister and daughter. He is at peace with the world.

3. Shankara's Secret

Without empathy there is no evolution

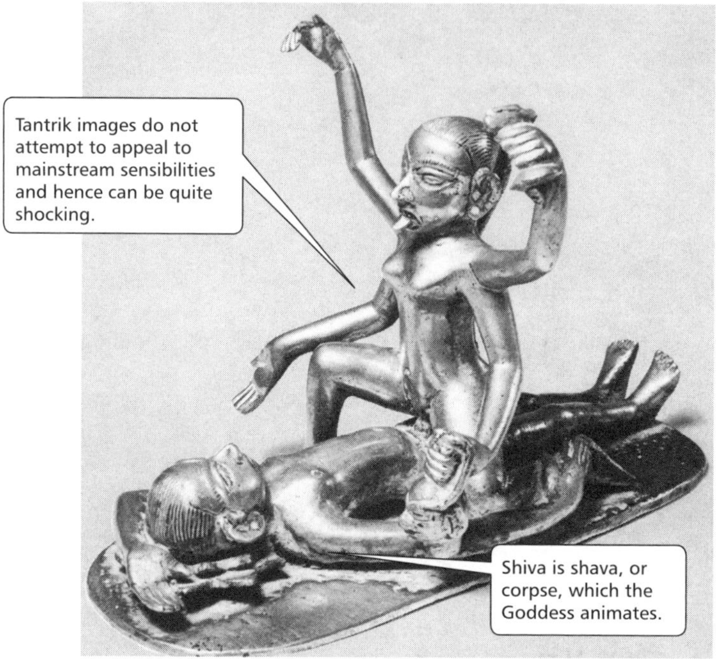

Tantrik imagery showing Kali forcing an indifferent Shiva to copulate

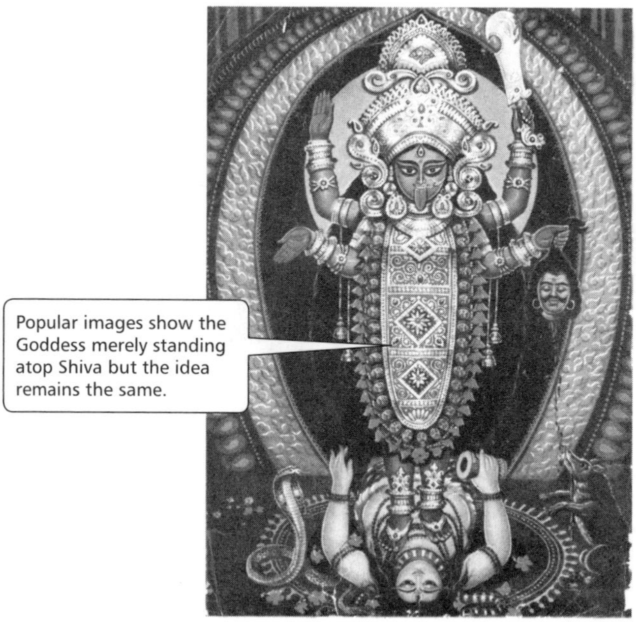

Poster art showing Kali standing atop Shiva, forcing him to awaken

Shiva is Rudra, the angry god. He is angry with Brahma because Brahma seeks freedom from fear by trying to control Prakriti rather than by seeking Purusha. In anger, he beheads Brahma, then shuts his eyes and immerses himself in the infinite bliss of an unfettered consciousness, sat-chitta-ananda. Liberated from all things sensory, nature has no effect on him.

Physics informs us that a surface looks white when all the colours in the light spectrum are reflected back. Shiva reflects back all things material. He holds on to nothing. To him, everything is as ephemeral as camphor. That is why he is called Karpura Gauranga, he who is as white as camphor.

But what is the point of wisdom if divorced from the world? Wisdom is meaningless if it does not enable the liberation of those who are trapped in fear. That is why the Goddess stands in opposition of Shiva as both the radiant Gauri, producing light, and as the dark Kali, consuming light. While Shiva sits still in the north, she comes forth swaying from the south as Dakshina-Kali, demanding to be seen. Nature will not be ignored.

The Goddess is naked with hair untied and drinks blood. Her nakedness is an invitation to sex, hence to childbirth and life. Her lust for blood is her acceptance of death. She is both life and death. Her unbound hair is a reminder that she is wild and raw. She is Shakti, energy, constantly on the move. He, on the other hand, is still like the hooded cobra. He shuts his eyes to her.

In Indian philosophy, a thing exists when it is seen. And a creature is alive when it sees. Shiva's eyes are shut, meaning he is indifferent to the fears of those around him. Shakti, the mother,

Shiva with the Goddess who holds up a mirror

will not allow that. If she is Bhairavi, inducing fear, she needs Bhairava to enable the frightened to outgrow fear. Without Shiva, Brahma will remain finite and never realise his divine potential.

Brahma's eyes are open, but he sees only his own fears, not those of others around him. Consumed by his own Brahmanda, he does not realise each one of those around him has a Brahmanda of his or her own. He needs to look at others, recognise that every man and every woman has his or her own subjective reality, his or her own unique way of looking at the world. He needs to have empathy.

Looking at others is called darshan. Brahma looks at others in fear: he pursues them as he pursues Shatarupa. He seeks them when they comfort him; he shuns them if they frighten him. When he looks at them, he wonders if they are 'mine' or 'not mine'. A gaze that is born of fear, a gaze that excludes and exploits is not darshan. Darshan is gaze that is free of fear. Darshan is gaze that looks at the other for its own sake not because it is 'mine' or 'not mine'. Darshan is an empathy-filled gaze. We see people around us as deer who fear predators, or as lions who fear scarcity and seek prey, or as dogs who bark when threatened or whine when ignored. Darshan enables us to see people's thinking patterns or mind-sets. We recognise the Brahma and identify the Brahmanda around them. We see the pashu – dependent on Prakriti, frightened of Yama, lacking faith in atma and seeking refuge in aham.

When we genuinely do darshan, we discover how the other reacts to us. That is, the other ends up as a mirror or darpan, reflecting who we are. If people around us behave like deer, it means we are behaving like lions. If people around us behave like lions, it means they see us as deer. If people around us behave like dogs, friendly or hostile, it means we matter to them.

South Indian stone sculpture showing Shiva as Pinaki, the bearer of the bow

The Goddess wants humans to look at humans as humans. This will not happen as long as fear governs the relationship. Simply cutting Brahma's head will not remedy the situation. Some hand-holding is required. Just as Brahma needs to have faith in Shiva, Shiva needs to have patience with Brahma. For this, Shiva has to first engage with the world, not withdraw from it. Determined to get Pashu-pati to help humans, Shakti dances on top of him. She hopes to transform Shiva, the insensitive, angry god, into Shankara, the god who empathises and is patient.

In the lore of Shiva, Brahma is treated as Shakti's father and Shiva is her beloved. Brahma behaves as a father should not behave, when he seeks to control his daughter. For this act, Shiva beheads him. Shiva behaves as a beloved should not behave, when he shuts his eyes to Shakti. The Goddess negotiates with both father and beloved. The father needs to trust and the beloved needs to pay attention. A relationship is needed for harmony to exist.

The Puranas inform us that Brahma gives birth to 'mind-born' sons, which means sons created without copulating with a woman. This is a metaphor for mental modification, a twisting and folding of the pristine imagination as it experiences more and more fear. One of these sons is called Daksha, the skilled one. His name alludes to Dakshin, the south, the land of movement, birth and death. The birth of Daksha is Brahma's response to nature.

Daksha also means the skilled one. He is skilled at coping with nature's transformation. He does so by establishing culture through the ritual of yagna.

Yagna is all about controlling wild nature and domesticating

Daksha performing a yagna

it so that it comes under human control, becomes manageable, predictable, hence less frightening. Yagna is a metaphor for domestication. Yagna involves domestication of fire, limiting it to a sacrificial altar. Yagna involves domestication of water, limiting it to a pot. Yagna involves domestication of plants and animals; some become auspicious offerings while others remain inauspicious outsiders. Yagna involves domestication of humans through rules, regulations and rituals; everyone has a different role and responsibility with respect to the ritual, hence to society. Yagna thus transforms forest into field, wild animals into pets and beasts of burden, man into husband, woman into wife, and humans to members of castes, clans and communities. Yagna thus creates hierarchy. And, therefore, the *Rig Veda* holds yagna as the core of human activity. It refers to society as a human organism, or Purusha. It refers to dismemberment of this Purusha as hierarchies are established and humans are classified and differentiated.

Through Daksha, Brahma becomes domesticator of nature and creator of culture. In exchange for domestication, yagna grants abundance and security and so promises the end of fear.

But end of fear for whom? Daksha is Praja-pati, master of the people. He is not Pashu-pati, master of animal instincts. Daksha seeks to dominate people around him rather than outgrow his own fears. His gaze is outward not inward. He seeks to control nature around him in order to feel secure. He seeks to domesticate everyone around him. He is not willing to question his own delusions which cause the amplification of his own fears. He is the alpha male, no different from the lion in the jungle that uses force to dominate and control his pride of lionesses. He remains pashu.

Poster art of Chandra, the moon-god

The moon in final phase of waning sits on Shiva's head

Daksha finds nature inhabited by two sets of divine beings: the Devas who live in the sky and the Asuras who live under the earth. Under the earth, withheld by Asuras, is all the wealth that society needs — plants and metals. The Devas provide the wherewithal — heat, light, wind, fire, rain — to draw this subterranean wealth out. With the help of the Devas, Daksha gets access to wealth hoarded by the Asuras. For Daksha, Devas are therefore 'gods' while Asuras are 'demons'.

Yagna is the ritual performed to make the Devas stronger so as to defeat and kill Asuras. Daksha establishes a relationship with the Devas by offering them his daughters as their wives. This is a transactional relationship. If either the Devas or his daughters do not comply with this arrangement, he loses his temper.

Daksha gives twenty-eight of his daughters, the Nakshatras, to Chandra, the moon-god. The moon, however, prefers only one of them, Rohini, lavishing her with attention while neglecting the others. Upset, one of the Nakshatras, Abhijit, withers away in sorrow, while the other twenty-six daughters complain to Daksha, who curses Chandra to suffer from the wasting disease. As the days pass, Chandra starts to wane, much to Daksha's satisfaction. A distraught Chandra turns to Shiva, the god who defeats Yama. Shiva, who is Mrityunjaya, conqueror of death, places Chandra on his forehead. This contact enables Chandra to wax once again, much to Daksha's irritation. Shiva is therefore known as Chandrashekhara, on whose head sits the moon.

Daksha takes the life of one who does not align to his rules; Shiva gives life instead and expects nothing in return, least of all

North Indian painting showing Sati with Shiva

obedience. The Devas therefore call Shiva Maha-deva, the greatest of gods, he who is God, hence independent of nature's laws.

Daksha does not consider Shiva to be Maha-deva. He views Shiva as the enemy who opposes him. Shiva seems to side with the Asuras by giving their guru, Shukra, the secret knowledge of resurrection known as Sanjivani Vidya. Using Sanjivani Vidya, Shukra is able to bring back to life all the Asuras killed by the Devas. That is why, much to Daksha's exasperation, wild nature cannot be permanently domesticated. Eventually fields and orchards are overrun by weeds and forests season after season, children of domesticated animals remain wild and have to be broken generation after generation, rules once instituted have to be reinforced year after year. Yagnas have to be performed again and again to keep intact the crucible of culture.

What Daksha fails to realise is that Shiva does not distinguish between Devas and Asuras; he is indifferent to their station or their roles. One is not the hero and the other is not the villain. Shiva does not share the prejudices that shape Daksha's thoughts.

For Daksha, obedience is virtue. He excludes those who do not obey him. Asuras do not obey him, Chandra does not obey him, Shiva does not obey him. Asuras are therefore sacrificed during the yagna; Chandra is tolerated only when he agrees to share his attention between all his wives; but Shiva is always excluded, as Shiva remains indifferent to him.

To Daksha's vexation, his youngest daughter, Sati, disobeys him. One day she sees Shiva wandering in the mountains. She recognises him for who he is and falls in love with him. She expresses her

Manuscript painting of Bhairava

Temple wall carving of Bhairava

desire to be his wife. Her father refuses to grant permission but she is adamant. Shiva does not pay her any attention, but it does not deter her; she is in love. Daksha refuses to accept Shiva as his son-in-law and include him in his household. So Sati leaves her father's house to become Shiva's wife.

Rather than understanding Sati, Daksha is angry. Sati's defiance makes him feel insignificant. So he refuses to acknowledge her independence. He blames Shiva for Sati's behaviour. To teach both Shiva and Sati a lesson, he conducts a grand yagna. All Devas are invited to Daksha's sacrificial hall to partake the sacrificial offerings. Everyone except Shiva and Sati are called. Through exclusion, Daksha seeks to teach both of them a lesson. He hopes to eventually domesticate them.

Shiva does not care. But Sati is upset. Why has she not been invited? Maybe it is just an oversight, she thinks, and insists on going back to her father's house. Shiva does not stop her. She comes of her own free will and she is leaving of her own free will. He simply says, 'The oversight is intentional.' Sati does not listen.

When she enters the sacrificial hall, she expects to be greeted by her loving father. Instead she is humiliated. 'Why have you come? You were not called,' says Daksha. Sati demands to know why Shiva has not been invited. He is also a son-in-law, one even the Devas respect. Daksha snarls, 'I will not invite a man who does not care for culture and who is even indifferent to nature. Look at him. He wanders around naked, smears his body with ash, smokes narcotics, dances in crematoriums, takes refuge in caves and mountains, has no home, has dogs and ghosts and snakes as his companions. He is filthy and vile and disgusting and unworthy of any sacrificial offering. He is not welcome in my house. And if

South Indian temple wall image of Virabhadra attacking Daksha you have any shame, you will stay out too.'

Sati knows that her father's insults do not matter to her husband. Daksha seeks control; Shiva lives in freedom. But she wants her father to see sense, recognise the Maha-deva, the god who gives life. She also wants her husband to see sense, realise that engaging with Daksha is critical. How else will Daksha outgrow his desire for control? How else will Daksha outgrow his fears? How else will Praja-pati understand Pashu-pati?

So Sati leaps into the sacrificial fire and sets herself ablaze. She makes herself the offering to the one who is denied offering by Daksha. She burns for Shiva.

When Sati follows Shiva, she does it out of unconditional love. She does not expect him to change. She serves him without asking anything in return. Shiva remains the wandering Tapasvin. She accepts him as he is. This is why the word 'sati' means a devoted wife.

But Sati's unquestioning, undemanding company dents Shiva's indifference. Following her self-immolation, he is forced to look at her. He does Sati's darshan – finds a charred corpse in the sacrificial altar. Sati becomes his mirror, his darpan. Her painful death is a reflection of his indifference and her father's fear of her independence. When he learns that no one came to her rescue, he realises how much fear governs the world of Praja-pati, making people submit to the most unreasonable demands. He decides to show Praja-pati a fear greater than all others fears. His righteous outrage takes the form of Virabhadra, a terrifying warrior.

Virabhadra leads an army of ghosts and goblins, of Ganas and

Modern sculpture of Shiva with the body of Sati

South Indian painting of Daksha with the head of a goat

Pramathas, all inauspicious and wild creatures, into Daksha's sacrificial hall and goes about destroying the precinct. Everything that is holy is rendered unholy. Urine, sputum, blood and vomit are poured into the pots and pans. Screams and shouts and cackles replace the melodious hymns. Order is disrupted. The guests run and scream in fear. There is chaos and cacophony. Dogs howl. Ghosts screech. Virabhadra finally finds Daksha and beheads him.

As Virabhadra, Shiva beheads Daksha just as he had beheaded Brahma in the form of Kapalika. The severing of the creator's head is a recurring theme in Hindu mythology. This follows the abuse of the Goddess. Brahma lusts for Shatarupa and Daksha insults Sati. With the act of beheading, Shiva condemns the misuse of the human mind to control and domesticate nature and to create a self-image that deludes one to justify such action. Rather than exploring the possibility of outgrowing fear, humans are indulging animal instincts. Rather than discovering the infinite, humans are choosing to entrap themselves in the finite.

Shiva lifts the corpse of Sati in his arms and wanders the hills, howling in pain. In sorrow, even Shiva forgets that he who can restore Chandra, he who can give Sanjivani Vidya to the Asuras, can resurrect anyone. Indifferent to her all her life, Shiva misses her in death and so experiences pain and weeps. His howling is so intense that the universe is unable to bear its burden. So Vishnu hurls his discus, the Sudarshan Chakra, and cuts Sati's body into 108 pieces. Each piece falls on earth and transforms into a Shakti-pitha, the seat of the Goddess.

With the body gone, Shiva regains his composure. The Devas beg him to forgive Daksha. They beg him to resurrect Daksha so that the yagna is not left unfinished. Shiva replaces Daksha's head

Miniature Indian painting of Kama

with that of a male goat, which was supposed to be the sacrificial offering. Symbolically, he reminds Daksha what true sacrifice is — the sacrifice of one's animal nature and the realisation of one's human nature. Only then will Praja-pati become Pashu-pati. Only then will fear give way to tranquillity.

Shiva then withdraws to his mountain of snow under the Pole Star. He withdraws into a cave. Like a turtle, his senses once again stop engaging with Prakriti. The endless pillar of fuel-less fire burns again.

The story is far from over as far as the Goddess is concerned. This is merely part one of a two-act play. In Prakriti, death is merely a comma, not a full stop. What goes around always comes around. What went away as Sati will surely return, but embodied in a different form.

As Sati, the Goddess has opened Shiva's heart to feeling. He experiences loss and reacts with passion. But now the Goddess wants his engagement with the world to be more considered, emerging out of concern and affection, not rage. Only then will Shiva truly be Shankara.

So the Goddess takes birth as Parvati, daughter of Himavan, king of mountains. Shiva's abode, Kailasa, is located atop Himalaya, the abode of snow. That is her father's kingdom. He is her father's guest. Just like Sati in her previous life, Parvati decides Shiva shall be her husband. He may be an avowed hermit, but she will make him a householder.

To help Parvati awaken Shiva, the Devas enlist the help of Kama, the god of desire. They tell him to shoot his arrows at Shiva when

Poster art showing Shiva setting Kama aflame

the Goddess approaches him.

Kama is described as a cheerful god who rides a parrot and has as his weapon a bow whose shaft is made of sugar cane and string made of bees. His arrows are made of flowers with which he stirs the five senses. His companions are Vasanta, god of spring, and Rati, the goddess of lovemaking. His entourage is made up of Apsaras, dancing damsels, and Gandharvas, celestial musicians. They hold aloft his banner, which displays his symbol, the Makara, the constellation Capricorn. When the sun enters this constellation, winter gives way to spring, the cold earth is warmed with desire and, like a flower, opens itself to the sky.

With the aid of Kama, Indra has managed to destroy the tapasya of many a Tapasvin. Kama's arrows have made upward flowing semen of hermits flow downwards. Rather than igniting tapa in their minds and throwing light on Purusha, it has flowed out into Prakriti to create a child. They have thus been fettered by nature and denied liberation.

Shiva, however, is no ordinary Tapasvin. He is the Purusha. He is Pashu-pati. When Kama shoots his arrows, Shiva remains unaffected. He simply opens his third eye. Out comes a missile of flames and sets Kama ablaze. Rati and Parvati watch in horror as Kama is reduced to ashes. Shiva remains as tranquil as ever. The phallus remains self-stirred and his eyes remain shut. He remains indifferent to Prakriti. By this act, Yamantaka, the destroyer of death, also becomes Kamantaka, the destroyer of desire, hence life.

The third eye of Shiva indicates transcendental wisdom. Implicit in the idea of desire, is the idea of choice. Desire means the quest

Stone carvings from Southeast Asia and north India showing Parvati meditating

Poster art showing Shiva appearing before Parvati

for one thing over another. To want something one must not want another thing. In other words, one needs two eyes, one that selects and the other that rejects. When both eyes are shut it means nothing is selected or rejected, nothing is approved or disapproved, nothing is included or excluded. Everything is the same. The third eye therefore embodies absence of discrimination and choice, hence absence of desire. Kama is unable to open Shiva's two eyes. He succumbs to Shiva's third eye. Parvati, however, refuses to accept defeat. She is determined to make Shiva open his two eyes — not by force or cunning, as Kama tries to do, but by his own volition.

Parvati, a princess of the mountains, decides to turn to tapasya to awaken the Tapasvin. She rejects her colourful clothes, her jewellery, her cosmetics, drapes herself in bark and proceeds to invoke Shiva. She prays to him with single-minded devotion, standing on one toe in the cold, immersing herself in freezing water, surrounding herself with fire. She does not eat or drink. She tortures her body to demonstrate her determination and her devotion. She becomes the Tapasvini.

Parvati's austerities form the root of the ritual known as vrata, during which women of the household fast and stay awake all night hoping to change the fortunes of their household and bring in luck and health and prosperity. In life, all circumstances are determined by karma. Every event in our life is determined by past actions. So every moment is as it is supposed to be. But it is possible to change one's fate and fortunes. The dance of Prakriti can change if Purusha intervenes. For that, one has to invoke Purusha through acts of determination that demonstrate desire and devotion.

Parvati is as firm as the mountain she is born of. Her determination is a measure of her devotion and her devotion

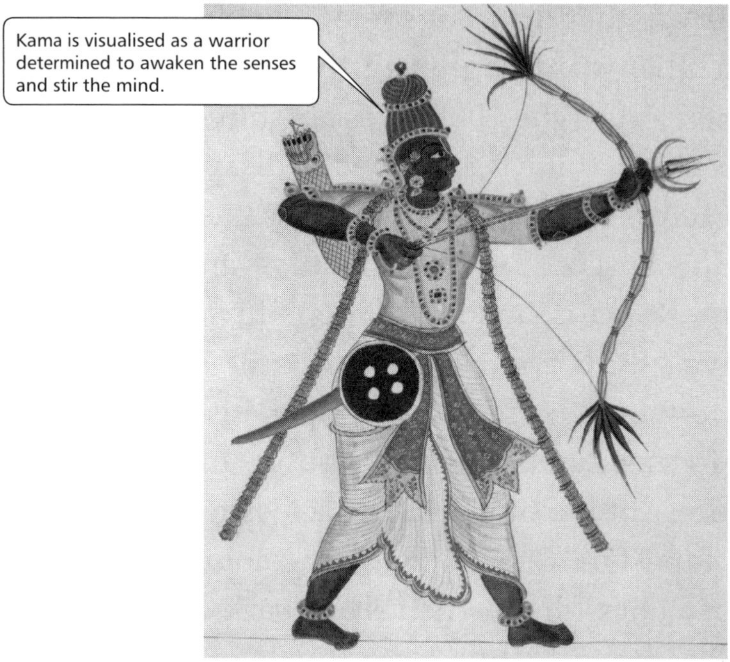

Mysore painting of Kama

Poster art of Kamakshi

stems from desire. She desires Shiva. She wants him to open his eyes. She wants him to embrace her and engage with the world. She wants to shatter his indifference.

Parvati's tapasya is different from that of other Tapasvins. Many Asuras and Devas and Rishis like Markandeya perform tapasya and invoke God. They ask for boons that benefit themselves. Parvati seeks from Shiva a boon that benefits others. She wants Shiva not for her pleasure but for the benefit of the world. Through her austerities she hopes to evoke compassion and empathy in his heart. Without him, all living creatures are fettered to nature. He will liberate them. They are bound by gravity; he will release them with his grace.

In the *Shiva Purana*, it is said that Parvati's actions stir Shiva. He opens his eyes and moves towards her. At first he tests her resolve. 'Are you sure you want to marry a wandering mendicant, a good-for-nothing vagabond?' Parvati says yes. 'Don't you want a more worthy groom? A more handsome, stronger and richer groom?' Parvati says no. He tries to distract and dissuade her, but he fails.

So intense is Parvati's devotion that he finally succumbs. 'Ask and it shall be yours,' he says. She asks that he become her groom. He agrees. She asks that he come to her house and ask her father for her hand in marriage. She is not willing to run away from her father's house as she did in her last birth as Sati.

Shiva looks at Parvati and recognises Sati. If he shuts his eyes to her, she will once again transform into Kali, wild and fearsome. If he opens his eyes to her, she will become the gentle and demure Gauri. The world is frightening when nature is seen without wisdom; the world is beautiful when nature is seen through wisdom. Parvati holds her mirror to Shiva, and Shiva finds himself reflected in it as the attentive Shankara.

Mysore painting of gods at the court of Shiva and Parvati

Poster art showing Shiva's marriage

And so Shiva comes on his bull with his Ganas to the abode of Himavan and asks for Parvati's hand in marriage. It is given, and she goes to Kailasa with him as his wife with her father's blessing. Thus is Shiva domesticated by Shakti. The hermit turns into Shankara, the householder. The Goddess is therefore called Kamakshi or Kamakhya, she in whose eyes resides Kama. She is visualised as holding in her hands all the symbols associated with Kama: the sugar cane, flowers and parrot. In her body, Kama is reborn but qualified with devotion.

Shiva refuses to respond to lust. That is why Kama fails. Shiva responds to prayer. That is why Kamakshi succeeds. She does not force Shiva to engage with the world; she beseeches him to do so. Unlike Sati who followed him rejecting her father, Parvati insists that he come to her and seek approval of her father. The relationship of Shiva, Sati and Daksha is a negative one with an indifferent husband and an angry father. The relationship of Shankara, Parvati and Himavan is a positive one, with a concerned husband and a loving father.

Had Kama established the relationship between Shiva and Parvati, it would have been a relationship based on power between the temptress (Parvati) and the tempted (Shiva); it would have been the reverse of the relationship between Brahma, who seeks to conquer, and Shatarupa, who refuses to be conquered. The relationship between Shiva and Parvati is not based on power. There is no conqueror and there is no conquest. Each one allows the other to dominate. Neither seeks to dominate the other. This is love.

Bengali Kalighat painting of Shiva as half Goddess

In south India, the marriage of Shiva and Shakti turns the Goddess from a wild warrior woman into a demure consort. The domestication is mutual. While he stops being a hermit, she stops being wild. He surrenders to become the householder, and she surrenders to be his wife. From the fearsome Bhairavi, she becomes the pretty Lalita, as Shiva transforms into Shankara.

After Shiva's marriage, Bhringi, a follower of Shiva, wanted to go around Shiva. Shiva said, 'You have to go around Shakti too. I am incomplete without her.' But Bhringi refused. He tried to slip in between the God and the Goddess. So the Goddess sat on Shiva's thigh, making it difficult for Bhringi to pass between the two. Bhringi then took the form of a bee, intending to fly through the gap between their necks, thus completing his round of Shiva and excluding Shakti. Shiva then merged his body with Shakti. He became Ardhanareshwara, God who is half-woman, making it impossible for Bhringi to make his way between the two. Shakti cursed Bhringi that he would lose all parts of the body that come from the mother — the soft flesh and fluid blood. Bhringi was reduced to bones and nerves, parts that come from his father. Bhringi could not stand up as a result of this. So Shiva gave him a third leg. This Gana made of bones and stripped of flesh stands like a tripod next to Shiva and Shakti to remind the world that Shiva cannot be acknowledged without acknowledging the Goddess. By making Shakti half his body, Shiva declares to the world he is indeed Shankara, who empathises with the imperfections of worldly life.

In Shiva temples, Shiva cannot be worshipped without

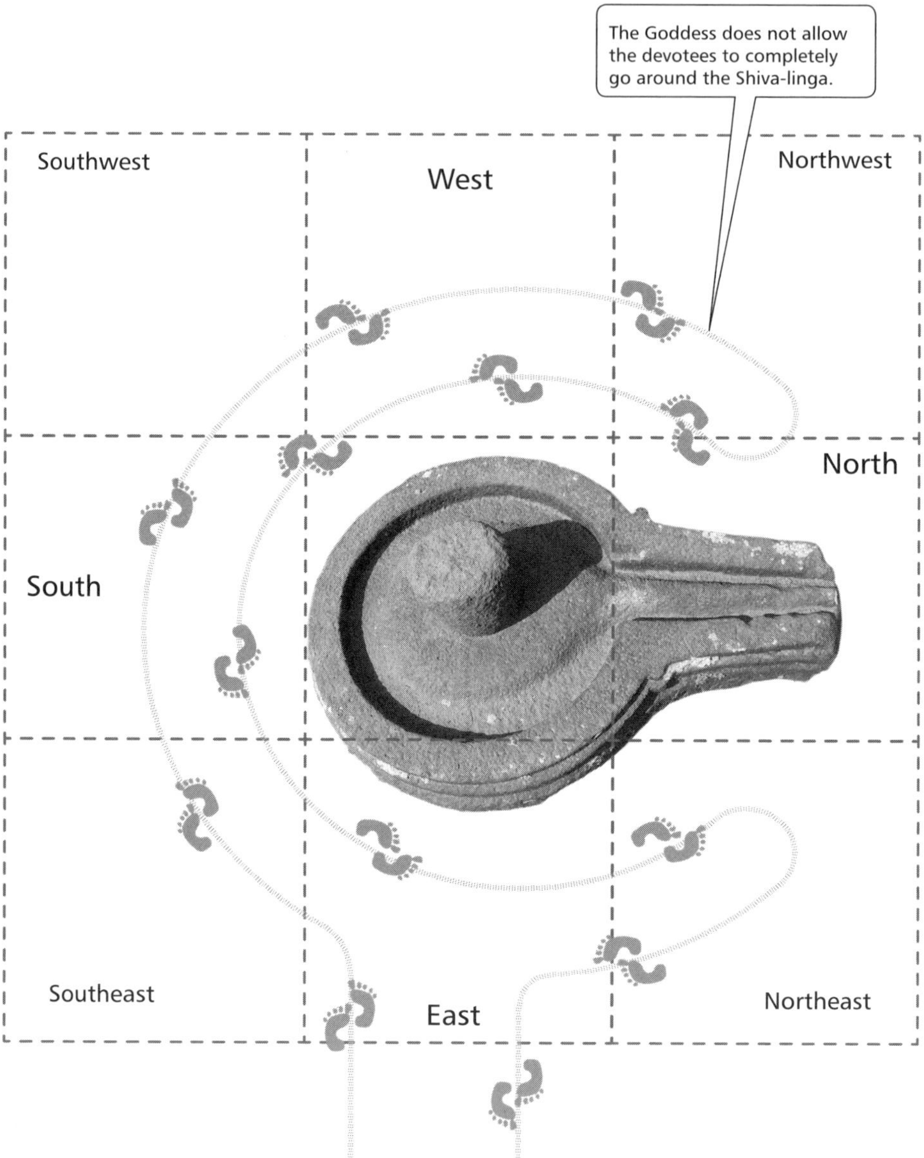

Shiva-linga and the directions

acknowledging the Goddess. The linga stone rises from a leaf-shaped trough that points north towards the Pole Star. This is the yoni, the entrance to the womb of the Goddess. The temple, or garbha griha, is the container of the womb into which Shiva has been drawn. She envelops him. Only through her can he be realised. Neither imagination, nor the wisdom that bursts out of it, has any meaning without nature. Wisdom exists for the world. Shiva and Shakti thus form one single unit.

One can go around the Shiva-linga but not completely; the circular path around is blocked by the tip of the trough. After moving clockwise, one has to turn around and move back around the linga once again in the counter-clockwise direction. Thus in a Shiva temple, the devotee moves from northeast to northwest and northwest to northeast, always traversing the south but never the north, a reminder that to reach Pashu-pati one has to live in the realm of Praja-pati. This realm is imperfect and frightening. Here, people often succumb to fears. But Shiva will not abandon them. Coaxed by Shakti, he will patiently wait for man to outgrow these fears until the river that flows southwards will turn to move northwards, pass through Kashi and eventually reach Kailasa.

4. Bholenath's Secret

Culture is a human delusion

North Indian Tantrik miniature painting of Kali on top of Shiva

South Indian poster art showing Shakti sitting on Shiva

In nature, animals have sex in the mating season to procreate. It is an instinct that ensures survival, governed by hormones and an internal clock. It is not a choice and it is not accompanied by an orgasm. Only in humans is sex a choice and a pleasure-seeking activity that need not culminate in procreation. Shiva is immortal, so does not need to procreate. Shiva is in a state of eternal bliss and so does not seek pleasure-seeking activities. He needs nothing and wants nothing. He is therefore autonomous, independent of nature. So when Shiva opens his eyes and accepts the Goddess, he does so out of grace. But being ignorant of worldly ways, he does not know how to make love to her. So the Goddess sits on top of him and guides him in the ways of the world.

One day, a group of sages paid a visit to Mount Kailasa and found Shakti on top of Shiva. An embarrassed Shakti covered her face with a lotus flower. Shiva, however, innocent of worldly ways, experienced no shame or embarrassment and continued as before. The sages were shocked. They realised Shiva did not intend to shock them: he simply did not know that his behaviour was socially inappropriate. He was ignorant. More appropriately, he was innocent. His mind was pure, untouched by demands of society. They declared he was Bhole-nath, the master who has no guile. He was the simpleton sage.

But culture is neither innocent nor ignorant. Culture's rules and prejudices would not look upon Shiva's activity favourably. It would embarrass, discomfort and confuse devotees. So the sages declared that no one would see Shakti and Shiva locked in intimate embrace, through which the Goddess sought to get Shiva to engage

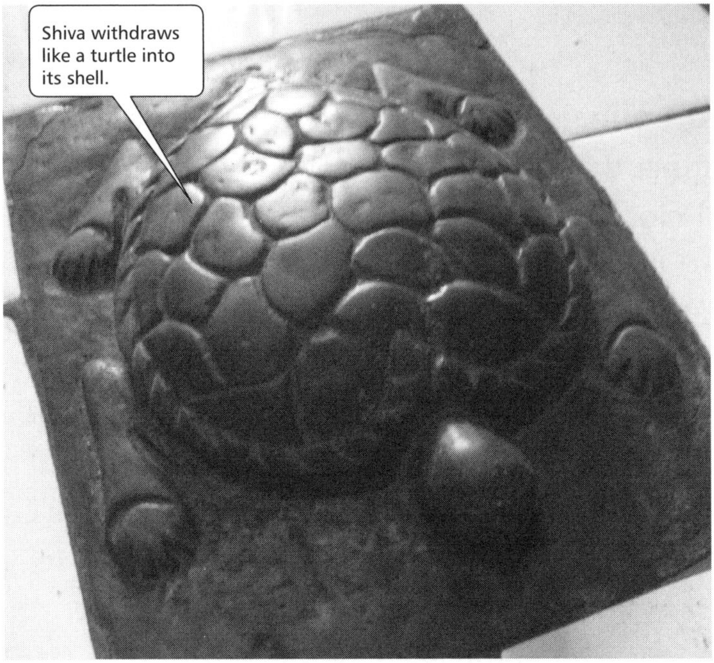

Turtle in front of Shiva temple

Dripping pot above Shiva-linga

with the world. Instead, this embrace would be visualised as a symbol. That is why the divine couple is worshipped as a linga-yoni combine.

Like the turtle placed before the Shiva-linga, Shiva seeks to slip away into his shell. So the Goddess has to work hard to keep his eyes open and his attention focused on the affairs of man. She turns into a pot that hangs above Shiva. The dripping water from the hole in the base ensures that Shiva does not slip into a trance, and that he is forever gracing his devotees with his benevolent gaze. He is like the hooded serpent: still, alert and aware of those before him. The water dripping from the pot is a reminder that time is running out; as water slowly drains out of the pot, breath is draining out of our body. We have but this lifetime as a human being to discover Purusha, or we will remain pashu despite being blessed with human imagination.

Shiva does not seek to defy or deny the value of cultural rules, rites and rituals. He is simply ignorant of them. He is not a rebel; he is simple and pure. This is most evident during the marriage of Shiva and Parvati.

Parvati insists that Shiva come to her house like a groom and ask her father for her hand in marriage. When her mother, Mena, and her sisters, step out to welcome the groom, the sight that awaits them horrifies them.

Unlike normal grooms who come on a mare, Shiva comes on a bull. Instead of being draped in fine cloth and sandal paste, he comes wrapped in animal hide and smeared with ash. Instead of garlands round his neck, he has serpents. Instead of bearing

North Indian Pahari miniature painting of Shiva's wedding procession

South Indian temple carving showing Parvati seeking Shiva's empathy

a sword, he holds in his hand a trident. Music is created not by flutes but by rattle-drums. His attendants are demons and ghosts and goblins and witches, Ganas and Pramathas and Yakshas and Bhutas. They have claws and fangs and bloodshot eyes. Everyone, Shiva included, drinks bhang, narcotic hemp, not from cups but from skulls.

Shiva's wild, uncouth form can be either frightening or endearing. The frightening form is called Kala-Bhairava, or the dark one. This form of Shiva is offered alcohol in temples. The endearing form is called Gora-Bhairava, or the light one. This form of Shiva is offered milk and sweetmeats and is also known as Batuk Bhairava or Bholenath.

Parvati's mother, Mena, is disgusted by Shiva's uncouth form. Parvati's sisters and aunts make fun of her. Parvati's father, Himavan, cannot understand her daughter's choice of husband. He is a barbarian: a wild, uncouth hermit.

The Goddess realises the tension between her father and her groom. This had happened before when she was Sati and her father was Daksha. She goes to Shiva and falls at his feet and prays to him, 'They are not enlightened enough to understand who you are. But you are enlightened enough to understand where they come from. So only you can salvage this situation. Behave as they wish you to. Indulge them so that they acknowledge and accommodate you. Only when you engage with them will they eventually realise you.'

And so, Shiva, touched by Parvati's sensitivity to him and her family, decides to indulge the world. He transforms into Soma-sundara, the one who is as beautiful as the moon. Stripped of the ash and the snakes and the animal hide, smeared with perfumes

Nandi, Shiva's bull, in a temple

Kalamkari painting of Shiva and Parvati on Nandi

Stone image of Shiva and Parvati on Nandi

and covered with silks, he is the most handsome man anyone has ever seen, graceful and lithe, regal in bearing. In this form, he asks the king of the mountains for Parvati's hand in marriage. It is given. Everyone rejoices at the wedding of Shiva and Shakti. It is the one occasion where eternal enemies, Asuras and Devas, dance together.

The relationship between Shiva and Parvati is best represented by Shiva's vehicle, the bull, Nandi.

To domesticate a bull, he has to be castrated. The absence of gonads deprives the animal of the male hormones that make him aggressive. He then becomes the gentle bullock, a beast of burden, who can serve society by pulling ploughs and carts. A bullock may be domesticated, but he is unable to father children. To father children, one needs to keep the bull intact. An intact bull is wild and aggressive. It will copulate with cows so that they can give birth to the calf and provide milk. An intact bull cannot be tamed. It must be allowed to roam free for the sake of human prosperity.

Nandi the bull represents Shiva's autonomy and capability. Though Parvati sits beside Shiva, he cannot be fully domesticated. His power comes from his being wild. Through Parvati, Shiva engages with the world but never quite assimilates with it.

Shankara is not Vishnu. Shankara merely engages with Prakriti while Vishnu seeks to establish Sanskriti, a culture that is not based on fear. Vishnu participates in worldly affairs, takes mortal forms, and is part of culture. Shiva watches culture from afar and patiently waits for man to outgrow the beast within him. Stories about Vishnu are therefore located in time and space, in particular eras or

Poster art of the marriage of Shiva and Parvati

Dolls showing marriage of Shiva and Parvati

yugas, in particular cities (he is Ram of Ayodhya in Treta yuga and Krishna of Gokul in Dvapara yuga), while stories about Shiva are located outside time and space. Vishnu forges the path of dharma, which will enable humans to outgrow the beast within them even while being fruitful members of society. Shiva prescribes vairagya, renunciation of society itself. For Vishnu, culture is the springboard to outgrow the beast and discover humanity. For Shiva, culture is a delusion that distracts man from outgrowing the beast and discovering humanity. Though the means are different, the goal of dharma and vairagya are the same. They seek to transform Prajapati, he who commands over human society, into Pashu-pati, he who outgrows the animal within.

When Shiva and Shakti reached Mount Kailasa after their marriage, Shakti says, 'I want a house.' Bholenath wonders why. 'To protect us from the heat in summer,' she says. He offers her the cool shade of the banyan tree as an alternative. He simply does not understand the need for a house. 'What will protect us from the winter cold?' she asks, in an attempt to get some sense into him. He takes her to the crematorium and offers the warmth of the funeral pyre; there is not a single night when one cannot find a funeral pyre, he points out. 'And when it rains? No tree or pyre will shelter us then!' cries an exasperated Shakti, realising her husband is not getting the point. He takes her in his arms and flies above the clouds where it does not rain. This is how Shiva gets the name Jimuta-vahana, he who rides the clouds.

Amongst Shiva's followers are mendicants who seek to emulate Shiva's inability to be bound by anything cultural. Like Shiva, they

Cave wall carving of Shiva and Parvati on Kailasa

stay in crematoriums. Like Shiva, they eat anything that comes their way, even human flesh. While cannibalism is taboo in culture, it is not so in nature. Many animals eat members of their own species, and so Aghoras, as they seek complete disruption of social rules, indulge is such practices. They even indulge in sexual activities with the dead, and follow habits that society considers vile and inappropriate. The word ghora means frightening, while Aghora means one who is not frightening. From a cultural point of view, the Aghoras behave in a frighteningly subversive way as they reject all notions of propriety and auspiciousness. But the Aghoras do this not to frighten anyone. They seek to be indifferent to the cultural gaze. They are on a quest to break all social conditioning that divides the world into appropriate and inappropriate, auspicious and inauspicious. They seek to be as transcendental as Shiva.

But Shakti wants Shiva to be more domestic. She wants him to be a husband who builds a house for the wife. Shiva cannot appreciate Shakti's need for a house. He sees it as a burden, an attachment, a cause of misery, but he decides to indulge her, out of affection and respect. He asks Ravana to build her a house.

Ravana is the king of Rakshasas. Rakshasas are considered demons because, though they have the intelligence and discriminatory powers that humans possess, they willingly choose to follow the law of the jungle and deliberately seek to dominate and control everyone around them. Ravana's father is Vaishrava, whose father was Pulatsya, another mind-born son of Brahma. Thus, Ravana is a descendant of Brahma. Metaphorically speaking, Ravana then is a form of Brahma created when imagination is crumpled and knotted by several layers of fear.

While Brahma has five heads, one of which was wrenched off by

Stone sculpture from Chhattisgarh showing Ravana sacrificing his heads to Shiva

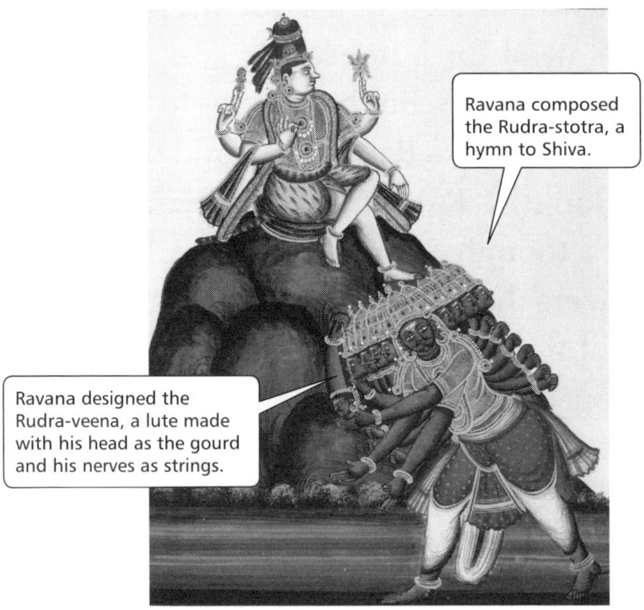

South Indian painting of Ravana and Shiva

Shiva, Ravana has ten. Ravana cuts these heads off and offers them to Shiva. He uses one of his heads and one of his hands to create a lute or veena. The head serves as the gourd of the lute while his hand serves as its beam and his nerves serve as its strings. This is the Rudra-veena, the lute that is offered to Shiva. It is also known as Ravan-haath, the hand of Ravana, and it is the inspiration for all stringed musical instruments of the world. Using this, Ravana sings a song in praise of Shiva. Shiva is pleased with Ravana's voluntary sacrifice of his heads, which metaphorically speaking, is the gradual uncrumpling and unknotting and purification of the mind. Being Bholenath, he does not wait for all heads to be cut. In his impatience to be generous, he concludes that Ravana is a truly wise devotee.

Ravana is a devotee, but he is not a wise devotee; rather, he is a clever devotee. He seeks from Shiva freedom from fear, not through faith, but through power. When Shiva asks Ravana to build a house for Shakti, Ravana uses his knowledge of Vastu-shastra, or the occult understanding of space, to build a grand palace. It turns out to be the most beautiful palace on earth. After building it, Ravana, becomes attached to it and covets it. So when Shiva says, 'How can I reward you for building such a good palace?', Ravana asks for the palace itself as his fee, and the simpleton Shiva says, 'So be it.' Shakti, who loves the palace and looks forward to turning it into her home, cannot believe it when Ravana declares that Shiva has gifted it away to him. Very cheekily, Ravana invites the Goddess to stay in the palace as a guest or tenant.

Shakti wants to be angry with Shiva but realises he has behaved according to his nature. He did not understand the concept of house or home or property. She has to accept him for what he is.

Ravana trying to raise Mount Kailasa on his head

Once, Ravana uproots Mount Kailasa, intent on taking it and its divine residents south to his island-kingdom of Lanka. Shiva does not mind but Shakti is upset. She requests Ravana to stop. Ravana refuses. 'I am mightier than Shiva. I can carry him, his wife and his home on my shoulders,' he declares. Hearing this, Shiva presses his big toe against the ground and creates such force that Ravana is crushed under its weight. Ravana apologises by singing hymns in praise of Shiva. Shiva, who is quick to anger, is also quick to forgive. So Ravana is forgiven.

Taking advantage of Shiva's gullible nature, the incorrigible Ravana once makes a request to Shiva, 'I want your wife to be my wife.' Shiva replies, 'If she wants to go with you, she is free to do so.' Being Bholenath, he does not understand notions of wife or spousal rights or marital fidelity. Shakti decides to teach the vile and cunning Rakshasa-king a lesson. She takes a frog or manduka and transforms her into a beautiful damsel called Mandodari and makes her sit atop Mount Kailasa. When Ravana reaches the mountain-top and sees this beautiful woman, he concludes it must be Parvati, wife of the hermit Shiva. He picks her up, takes her to Lanka, and makes her his queen. Shiva and Shakti watch with amusement as the demon-king makes love to the frog-woman, arrogantly believing he has tricked Shiva himself.

Shiva's apparent naïveté stems from great wisdom. He knows that power does not take away fear; it only fuels more fear. Shiva's line of sight is infinity; Ravana's line of sight is finite. Eventually, Ravana will realise the folly of his way. Eventually, the smart demon will realise he can never outsmart divinity.

Kerala mural showing Shiva with Mohini

South Indian painting of Mohini

As Shankara, Shiva bestows boons to anyone who approaches him. A blessing is offered even when the offering is accidental. Once a thief and murderer, running from soldiers, climbed a tree and spent the whole night there to avoid the gaze of his pursuers. He was atop a bilva tree and below the tree was a Shiva-linga. Without realising it, he dropped a few bilva leaves on the Shiva-linga. This was enough for Shiva to forgive the thief and murderer.

A woman called Draupadi once asked Shiva for a husband who is honest and strong and skilled and handsome and intelligent. Instead of giving her one husband with all five qualities, Shiva gave her five husbands each with one quality, without taking into consideration the cultural taboo against polyandry.

Culture by its very nature makes room for some practices and some people, and excludes others. Thieves and criminals and ghosts and goblins have no place in culture. But they all find refuge with Shiva. Shiva is surrounded by all manner of creatures that society deems to be demons. He sits with them, dances with them, and includes them. It is not that he excludes members of society, but members of society find it difficult to connect with a divinity who does not discriminate like them.

The Goddess has no choice but to put up with Shiva's behaviour. As nature, she is mother of all creatures. She understands why they are what they are. But she is also the daughter of culture, she knows why culture shuns such creatures. She struggles to negotiate a truce between the mainstream and the outsiders. But she knows that Shiva is who he is because he does not discriminate. He looks beyond the divisions of auspicious and inauspicious laid down by society.

Once an Asura asked Shiva for a boon. 'Let any creature on

Poster art showing Shiva drinking poison

South Indian art showing Parvati squeezing Shiva's neck

whom I place my hand turn into ash.' Shiva granted the boon only to discover that the Asura sought to place his hand on Shiva first. Shiva ran, not knowing how to tackle the foolish Asura. If Shiva is destroyed then the whole world is destroyed. But the Asura was not thinking about the world. He was only thinking about himself and how powerful he would be if he told the world how he destroyed Shiva. Shiva sought the help of the worldly-wise Vishnu, who took the form of a ravishing damsel called Mohini and enchanted the foolish Asura with her beguiling smile. One look at Mohini and the Asura forgot all about Shiva. 'Be my wife,' he begged her. Mohini said she would if he could dance just like her. She began dancing and the Asura imitated her steps. He moved his hands and legs and hips and head just like she did. At one point, she touched her head with her hand. So did he. And in an instant, he was reduced to ash. Thus the boon of Shiva worked against him.

The Asura represents ambitious humanity. Shiva has complete faith in humanity. Vishnu is wary of human cleverness that makes them do foolish things. Humanity therefore ends up inventing technologies and social structures that are short-sighted, hurting humans and nature. Vishnu tries to make humans eventually see the folly of their ways. Shiva, however, is unconcerned. Even if humans destroy themselves, Prakriti will always survive in one form or another, and with her, Purusha.

Shiva's distance from all things socially appropriate is reinforced by what is offered to him in temple rituals. He is offered flowers and fruit of the poisonous plant, dhatura, which is never grown in any house. His favourite drink and smoke is made from the leaves and

Mysore painting showing a devotee sacrificing his eye for Shiva flowers of Cannabis Indica, a narcotic that is considered illegal by most governments around the world. His choice of refreshments and companions are seen as disruptive. Society demands discipline and alignment to rules. Shiva does not see the point.

One day, Vishnu got the Devas and the Asuras to churn Amrita, the nectar of immortality, from the ocean of milk. During this exercise, the ocean spewed out many wonderful gifts that were claimed by the Devas and Asuras and Vishnu. Finally the ocean spat out vast quantities of poison known as Halahal. No one wanted this. So everyone prayed to Shiva, the gullible hermit, and begged him to receive it. Shiva did it with no qualms as he did not find any difference between Amrita and Halahal. As the lord of yoga, only he had the power to digest this dreadful poison.

Shakti, however, was angry at how Shiva was being treated by everyone. Like a protective and concerned wife, she squeezed Shiva's neck and did not let the poison go beyond his neck. The poison turned Shiva's neck blue, which is why he came to be known as Nila-kantha.

Shiva once told Parvati, 'It is not what I am offered. It is the emotion that accompanies it that matters to me.' The Tamil epic *Periyar Puranam* tells the story of a tribal youth called Tinnan who, every evening after the day's hunt, offered forest flowers to a Shiva-linga that he carried in his hair, water from a mountain stream that he carried in his mouth and meat of the day's hunt, after deboning it with his own hands. The same Shiva-linga was offered flowers and incense and ashes and milk and fruits in the manner prescribed in the scriptures. To test whose devotion was genuine, Shiva caused the Shiva-linga to sprout a pair of eyes. One of the eyes started to bleed. The priest ran away, believing this was a bad omen. Tinnan,

Poster art of the Nath Yogis

Mendicants of Shiva who live outside mainstream society

however, tried his best to control the bleeding. When he failed to control it, he cut his own eye and offered it to the linga. 'Now, that is genuine emotion,' said Shiva, welcoming Tinnan to Kailasa.

In her role as wife, Shakti asks Shiva many questions. She forces him to break his silence and reveal his wisdom. Many Hindu scriptures take the form of conversations between Shakti and Shiva. It is said that the Ramayana, written by the sage Valmiki, was narrated to Valmiki first by the sage Narada, who heard it from the bull Nandi, who overheard a conversation between Shakti and Shiva. The Yakshas overheard the conversations between Shakti and Shiva and transmitted it in the form of the *Brihad-Katha-Sagar*, the ocean of stories, the fountainhead of all fables that entertain children through the ages, throughout the world.

Once a fish overheard a conversation between Shiva and Parvati. The wisdom enabled him to break free from his animal form and be reborn as a human. He became known as Matsyendra-nath. He taught the Tantras to his students, the Naths and the Siddhas. That is why the Tantras are often written in the form of Shiva-Shakti conversations.

The Tantras are sometimes known as Agamas to differentiate them from the Vedas, which are known as Nigamas. The difference between Agamas and Nigamas is that Agamas focus on the worship of a deity with form, i.e. saguna brahman, while Nigamas focus on the worship of a formless deity, nirguna brahman. Agamas tend to be more exoteric and celebrate the tangible while Nigamas are esoteric and celebrate the intangible. Agamas give greater value to the emotions that are provoked by

North Indian miniature showing Shiva and Parvati playing dice

Dolls displayed in a south Indian household during Navaratri

the ritual while Nigamas give greater value to the intellectual decoding of the ritual. Agamas approach Prakriti first and then Purusha, while Nigamas approach Purusha first and then Prakriti. In Tantras, Goddess is Shakti or power, to be sought, while in Vedas, Goddess is Maya, delusion, to be transcended.

But often Shiva does not appreciate the inadequacies and limitations of humanity; that they do not have the same capacity and capability as he does. It is in human nature to get bored and restless. Humans struggle to keep their attention still and focused. Often Shakti yawns when Shiva is speaking. This makes him angry. He loses his temper and turns away from the Goddess, leaving the icy peaks of Kailasa and hiding in the daruka vana, the deodar forest. The Goddess then has to woo him back, sometimes by taking the form of seductive Kirata, or tribal woman.

Sometimes Shiva curses Shakti when she displays signs of indifference. Once, he curses her to be born on earth as a fisherwoman. He regrets the curse almost immediately. To bring her back, he takes the form of a fisherman and wins her hand by earning her admiration by catching a fish in the sea, a dangerous shark that threatens the livelihood of the fisherfolk.

Shakti teaches Bholenath to be more patient with human beings. Imagination has other uses besides introspection and wisdom. It allows for fun. And so together the divine couple creates games and dolls that help humanity pass the time. This is why the festivals of the Goddess, such as Diwali and Dussera, are associated with board games and dolls. Shiva looks at games and dolls with disdain; he equates it with the rattle-drum that entertains and distracts the monkey-mind. But Shakti sees them as invaluable tools to help humanity cope with life.

Elephant cave wall carving showing Shiva impaling Andhaka

One day, Parvati covers Shiva's eyes with her palms. The world is plunged in darkness. To get the sun to shine again, Shiva opens his third eye. So fiery is the glance of this eye that it causes Parvati's palms, placed over the left and right eye, to sweat. From this sweat is born a child called Andhaka, the one born in darkness. This child is given to a childless Asura. When Andhaka grows up he invokes Brahma and secures a boon, that he should not be defeated in battle unless he looks upon his own mother with eyes of lust. Andhaka, who does not know how he was created, goes about conquering the world. No one can defeat him in battle. He finally reaches Mount Kailasa and challenges Shiva to a duel. However, Shiva is lost in meditation and does not pay heed to the challenge. Andhaka climbs the mountain and sees Parvati sitting beside Shiva. He is filled with lust, little realising that he desires his own mother. Parvati begs Shiva to open his eyes and stop their son from doing the unthinkable. Shiva opens his eyes; with his trident he impales Andhaka and keeps him alive and impaled for a thousand years, draining him of blood until he is reduced to a bag of bones. Thus tortured, Andhaka realises that the woman he lusted for is actually his mother and that Shiva is his father. He apologises to the divine couple and is allowed to live as a Gana in Kailasa.

It is significant that Andhaka is born when the third eye is opened. The story draws attention to the limitations of the transcendental gaze. The left and right eyes represent a gaze that distinguishes between appropriate and inappropriate conduct. The third eye is indifferent to such distinctions. This eye of wisdom cannot be

Poster art showing Shiva ready to receive the descent of the celestial Ganga accommodated within culture because culture, by definition, is based on distinctions, demarcations and hierarchies, where some aspects of nature are included and others excluded. In culture, rules transform a woman into a wife, and a man into a husband. The transcendental gaze looks at all rules as artificial and hence delusions. Such a gaze is unable to distinguish between woman and wife. That is why Shiva does not feel awkward offering his wife to Ravana. That is why the child born of the third eye is unable to recognise his mother and overpower his incestuous designs.

Shiva, they say, is so innocent that he does not know the difference not only between woman and wife, but also between man and woman. And so when Vishnu takes the form of Mohini, he intimately hugs Mohini right in front of his wife. Both Vishnu and Parvati do not know how to tell Bholenath that such a display of affection is inappropriate in culture. At the same time, Bholenath forces them to question cultural norms itself: why is certain behaviour acceptable and other behaviour not, what is the basis of appropriateness, why should culture stay static, why should any human construction not change as the human gaze changes?

One day, Bhagirath invokes Brahma and begs him to allow the river Ganga, which flows in the sky as the Milky Way, to flow on earth. This was to enable Bhagirath's dead ancestors to be reborn. 'Everyone, even the vilest of human beings, deserves another chance,' he says. Brahma agrees and orders Ganga, a river-nymph, to descend from the starry skies. But the force of the falling river can destroy the earth. A frightened Bhagirath requests Shiva to break the fall of Ganga. Shiva agrees and stands under the falling Ganga. The proud and arrogant Ganga suddenly finds herself getting entangled in Shiva's mighty dreadlocks. The force of her

Temple wall images showing Shiva as Hara-Hari, merged with Vishnu, and as Ardha-nari, merged with Shakti waters are contained by Shiva's hair. Shiva becomes Gangadhara, bearer of Ganga. The mighty river then springs out of Shiva's top knot as a gentle stream ready to water the earth, cleanse the living and enable the dead to be reborn.

If Shiva's thick locks represent the power of spiritual reality, then Ganga's force represents the strength of material reality. Shiva contains Ganga's force and controls her flow so that she does not overwhelm the earth. Thus, Shiva's power is contained in his body and is transmitted to the world through the Ganga. In Shiva temples, therefore, water and milk are poured on the Shiva-linga, in the hope that they will absorb tapa from within Shiva and make it available to the world around him. Only when Shiva's tapa leaves his body will the snow around him melt, and the river flow. Shiva, who lived alone in snowy Kailasa, therefore sits as Shankara along with Gauri on the banks of the river Ganga in the city of Kashi.

5. Ganesha's Secret

Food alone does not satisfy hunger

South Indian bronze sculpture of Shiva as Gajantaka, the elephant-killer

As long as the lion is hungry, the deer is afraid. As soon as the lion is fed, it forgets its fear of scarcity and the deer no longer has to fear the predator. Food thus plays a fundamental role in allaying fear.

The elephant has access to a lot of food, thanks to its great size. And thanks to its size, it has no natural enemies. This makes the elephant the least frightened of all animals in the jungle. This makes the elephant a symbol of power. Its presence points to a rich ecosystem that is fertile and green and full of water, capable of supporting many human settlements. This makes the elephant a symbol of prosperity. Naturally, it is associated with Indra, king of the Devas, ruler of the sky and Lakshmi, goddess of wealth.

Shiva however kills the elephant. He is Gajantaka, slayer of the elephant, who flays the elephant alive, dances on its head, and wraps its skin around his body. Elephant skin is not easy to cure and tan; it is full of fat and blood and rots easily. Shiva drapes around his body this Gaja-charma or elephant-skin. This reinforces Shiva's desire to stay away from all things material. He wants to break free from nature. He does not want to even depend on Prakriti for food.

When Parvati goes about setting up her kitchen in Kailasa, Shiva does not see the point. He watches her collect fruits and vegetables and grain and spices in baskets. He watches her domesticate fire in the stove. He watches her collect water in a pot. He watches her get her pots and pans and spoons ready. Then he sneers, 'What is the point of food? Everything will one day die anyway.' In response, the Goddess instantly disappears along with her kitchen. Now there is no food in Kailasa. Shiva's Ganas weep. Food, they say, keeps

Calendar art of Shakti as Annapurna of Kashi offering Shiva food the hunger pangs away. Food, they say, with its many flavours and textures, excites the senses, and helps them experience the variety of nature. Food, they say, provides contentment and allows the mind to move away from fear. Shiva feels the pain of his Ganas. He experiences what they experience. He yearns for what they yearn. He realises that these needs and cravings of the body force him to think about mortality. From fear of death stems the yearning for immortality and this yearning for immortality eventually paves the path towards spirituality. If there is no food, there is no body, no engagement with Prakriti, no encounter with Kama or Yama, no feeling whatsoever. Shiva realises how food plays a key role in the human journey from Prakriti to Purusha. He sets forth in search of his wife. He finds her on the banks of the river Ganga, in the city of Kashi, as the Goddess Annapurna, providing food to all those who come to her. Shiva extends his begging bowl. The Goddess, with great affection, fills it with hot, flavoursome food.

As a reminder of the value of the Goddess and her kitchen, uncooked food in the form of nuts and raw milk is offered to the hermit Shiva of Kailasa, while the householder Shankara of Kashi is offered cooked food.

Hindus believe that when a person dies, Yama claims his physical body, or sthula sharira, and his mental body, or sukshma sharira, which animates the physical body. But there is a third body – the body of subconscious memories, full of fears and resulting prejudices, known as karana sharira, which outlives death. This body envelops the Purusha and prevents it from observing the true nature of Prakriti, and hence realising its true self. That is

Bronze of Shiva holding the trident

why, when a person dies, the karana sharira travels across the river Vaitarni and reaches the land of the dead where it resides as a Pitr. As long as the karana sharira exists, fear still exists and the Pitr is not able to reach Shiva's Kailasa where there is bliss forever. In order to reach Shiva's abode, one has to purge the karana sharira of all fears and prejudices. This can only be done in the land of the living. For this, one needs a human body that offers the wherewithal to imagine and reflect and choose. To obtain the human body, the Pitr have to be reborn. Once reborn, to sustain the flesh, they need food.

The scriptures state that every living creature is obligated to produce children to repay the debt they owe to their ancestors who gave them life. This is Pitr-rin. During funeral ceremonies, the Pitrs are offered balls of mashed rice. The balls represent the human body because, ultimately, food forms the building block of the flesh. By offering these balls to ancestors, the living assure the dead that they will produce children, enable the dead to regain sthula and sukshma sharira, and thus repay their debt.

The concept of debt is a cultural thought that forces the human male to produce children. This cultural thought is needed because, of all creatures on this planet, only human couples can choose whether to have children or not. In case of all other animals, procreation is fettered by natural rhythms, not free will. Even amongst humans, the male of the species has greater choice. The female of the human species can be forced to conceive a child, but the human male cannot be forced to make a woman pregnant. Even if aroused, he need not spill the seed in the womb. Thus he can take pleasure but not father a child. The concept of debt to ancestors or Pitr-rin is an integral part of culture aimed at preventing men from

Temple wall image from Belur, Karnataka, showing Shiva and Shakti on a bull

North Indian miniature showing Shiva and Shakti atop Mount Kailasa

becoming indifferent, self-absorbed hermits and forcing them to become householders, responsible for others.

When Parvati expresses her desire to be a mother, Shankara argues, 'I owe no debt to any ancestors, as I have no ancestors; I was never born, and I will not die, so I need no children who will help me be reborn.' When Parvati persists, Shankara walks away from her to meditate in serene isolation in the dense daruka vana, the deodar forest.

Here, children are a powerful metaphor for true involvement with the material world. Through marriage, the Goddess has managed to open the eye of Shiva. Shankara observes nature, but does not feel responsible for nature. The only way he will feel empathy for the world, is when he creates something in it. A child is therefore necessary.

Since Shiva refuses to give her a child, Parvati decides to create a child on her own. She anoints her body with a paste of turmeric and oil, then scrapes it off, collects the rubbings which have mingled with her sweat, and moulds out of it a doll into which she breathes life. This is her son, whom she calls Vinayaka, the one born without (vina) a man (nayaka). She tells her son to guard the gate of her house and not let anyone in.

Shiva, who had withdrawn from the Goddess following her repeated demands for a child, returns only to find his path to Kailasa blocked by a stranger. He asks the stranger to step aside. The stranger refuses. Shiva gets jealous as he wonders about the beautiful boy who blocks his path. He gets angry because the boy is strong enough to block his path. The boy reminds him of the

Calendar art showing the creation of Ganesha

territorial Brahma and Daksha. He decides to get rid of the obstacle that blocks his path to the Goddess.

So Shiva raises his trident and beheads the boy. The head of Vinayaka is destroyed. Shiva marches in triumphantly, covered with the boy's blood. When Parvati sees this, she screams and runs to the threshold of her house, where she finds the headless body of her son. She wails and unties her hair and beats her chest in agony. 'My son, my son. You killed my son.' She transforms from the gentle, demure Gauri into the dark and fearsome Kali. She becomes wild in her fury. Shiva trembles.

Shiva realises his insensitivity. In satisfying his own need for solitude, he did not consider Parvati's loneliness atop the snow-capped peaks of the Himalayas. He did not look at her; he did not do her darshan. Had he known her needs, he could have satisfied them or helped her outgrow them. But he did neither. Unless the self-contained engage with the needy, the needy will never learn how to become self-contained. Parvati's temper, her transformation from Gauri to Kali, served as a darpan or mirror, reflecting Shiva's indifference. What use is imagination, if it simply ignores and invalidates the other?

Vinayaka does not recognise Shiva. Shiva does not like this. The Goddess thus turns the table on Shiva through Vinayaka. All this time, Shiva had shut his eyes to Shakti. Through Vinayaka, Shakti shuts her eyes to Shiva. When humanity ignores imagination, there is no growth, no quest to outgrow fear, no desire for spiritual reality. Evolution does not happen. Spiritual reality remains undiscovered. Only the self matters; others remain invisible. In other words, humans stay animals.

Realising the value of Prakriti and of the head that has been

Calendar art showing Shiva and Parvati with their son, Ganesha destroyed, a considerate and caring Shankara decides to resurrect the boy. He orders his Ganas to fetch him the head of the first creature they encounter in the northern direction. The Ganas find an elephant. The *Brahmavaivarta Purana* says this elephant was Airavat, the mount of Indra. Others say it was one of the elephants that flanks Lakshmi. The head is placed on the severed neck of Vinayaka and he is brought back to life.

Shiva declares him to be his son and names him Ganesha, first amongst Ganas, and Ganapati, master of the Ganas. Until this moment, the Ganas followed Shiva, but Shiva was indifferent to their presence. But now, thanks to his tryst with Parvati and Vinayaka, he looks at the Ganas, becomes sensitive to them, understands their inadequacies, includes them in his vision, and provides them with a leader, his own son. Ganapati thus embodies Shiva's empathy for the trials and tribulations of humanity.

Most scholars agree that the cult of Ganesha had an independent origin and that it merged with the cult of Shiva later in history. In early Vedic scriptures, there are references to multiple malevolent beings called Vinayakas, some of whom have elephant heads. In later Puranic scriptures, there is one gentle elephant-headed being who becomes the child of Shiva and Shakti.

There are many stories of Ganesha's birth besides the one in which Shiva beheads Vinayaka. In one story, Ganesha is born when Shiva and Shakti make love taking the form of elephants. In another, Shiva creates a child of his own image for the pleasure of Shakti, but since he looks too much like the father, Shakti replaces his head with that of an elephant.

Patta painting of Ganesha from Odisha

The cult of Ganesha was the most popular in Maharashtra, especially under the patronage of Maratha kings. Scriptures such as *Ganesha Purana* and *Ganesha Upanishad* were written in the 18th century in adoration of Ganesha, describing him as self-created. He is associated with the earth's fertility as well as the arts and wisdom. He is also described as a warrior who kills demons. One of the demons he killed was resurrected and turned into a rat, or Mooshika, which is Ganesha's vehicle.

Though the son of a hermit, Ganesha's corpulent belly indicates great affluence. He is surrounded by abundance. He is often worshipped with Lakshmi, the goddess of wealth. He is associated with several fertility symbols such as rats, serpents and blades of grass. The population of rats rises rapidly soon after its numbers have been exterminated, indicating their fertility. Serpents also slough old skin for new, and are thus able to regenerate themselves. Grass grows back as soon as it is plucked. Regeneration is critical to survival. Regeneration compensates for losses incurred by death. A shepherd who loses sheep to a wolf depends on the ability of the other sheep to reproduce to make good his numbers. A farmer who has harvested the crop depends on the regeneration of earth's fertility to ensure he does not starve the next season. Ganesha's association with fertility symbols is an acknowledgment of the cycle of life that sustains material reality. In the material world, everything dies and is reborn. Rats, serpents and grass are very visible and potent symbols of this principle.

In rituals, Ganesha is often worshipped with two mothers. They are identified as the elder mother and the younger mother. In

Photograph showing Ganesha being worshipped with his two mothers

Photograph showing Ganesha being immersed in water

Goddess tradition, Shakti is often worshipped with a female companion, her sakhi, who is identified as her sister or her servant. Some identify the younger mother as Lakshmi, and others as Ganga. The identification of two women as mothers draws attention to the greater role played by the Goddess in the creation of Ganesha. She initiates his creation; Shiva completes it. Ganesha draws attention towards the value of nature, of food and of worldly life.

Ganesha is worshipped twice a year, before the spring and autumn harvest. The more popular of the two Ganesha festivals is the one that takes place after the rains, in autumn, when the earth is green. Ganesha is worshiped with his mother, Gauri. She is the earth and he is the vegetation born of her that sustains life on earth. Both festivals of Ganesha involve making of clay statues of Ganesha. These are worshipped with blades of grass for ten days and then immersed in water. Ganesha's image thus comes and goes in a cyclical way, a reminder of nature's cycles, of the seasons of sowing and harvest, of life and death.

In many parts of India, Ganesha is considered a bachelor god. They say he did not marry as no woman was as good as his mother. So he stands in the shade of the banana tree who is his mother. There is another story for Ganesha's association with the banana tree. No one wanted to marry a man with the head of an elephant. So, his mother draped a sari around a banana plant and gave it to Ganesha as his wife. This is the reason a banana plant with a sari is found next to Ganesha during Durga Puja, celebrated in autumn. She is called Kola-Bau, the matriarch of the clan.

The banana plant is a valuable source of nutrition, demanding

Image of Kola-Bau and Ganesha from a Durga pandal in Bengal

Image of Vyasa and Ganesha

hardly any maintenance, constantly regenerating itself to provide more fruit. The pith of the banana plant is also edible. And the leaves of the banana plant serve as disposable dishes on which food is served. The banana is thus the Goddess taking care of food so that Ganesha can focus on wisdom. Ganesha therefore serves as a scribe to help the sage Vyasa write down the epic, the Mahabharata. This story captures the essence of life's truth, balancing Shakti's kitchen and Shiva's meditation.

Ganesha broke one of his two tusks to use it as a stylus with which he could write the epic that Vyasa narrated. In another story, he broke the tusk to strike the moon when it made fun of his huge size. In still another story, this tusk is broken when he is fighting either Parashurama or Balarama, both forms of Vishnu. By breaking one of the tusks, Ganesha's masculinity is toned down. Though son of Shiva and Shakti, he is closer to his mother, hence nature, and worldly life.

In folklore, tusks are associated with pretension: elephants show one set of teeth while they eat with another set of teeth. By breaking off one of the tusks, Ganesha is breaking pretension. The tusks are symbols of aggressive power. Ganesha is breaking it so that strength is used only to defend and nourish, not dominate and exploit.

Ganesha's association with wisdom is endorsed by his association with the Muladhara Chakra in Tantra. Tantra is the technology for the finite Brahma to reach the infinite Shiva with the help of Shakti. This is visualised as the rise of a serpent, Kundalini, representing our wisdom. Tantra visualises this serpent as resting at the base of the spine and rising up through the spine to the brain. As the serpent rises, lotus flowers bloom in the form of chakras. The final chakra

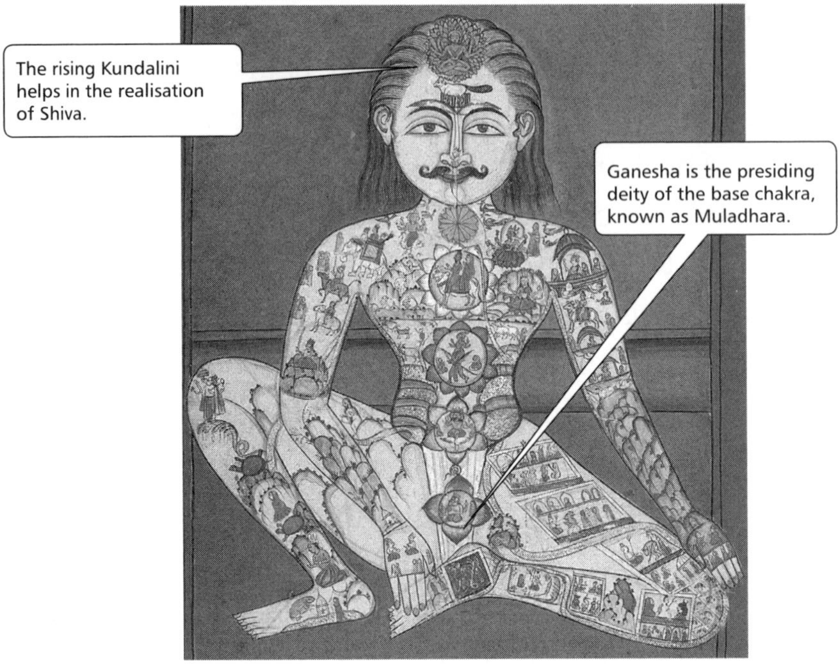

Seven chakras of Tantra

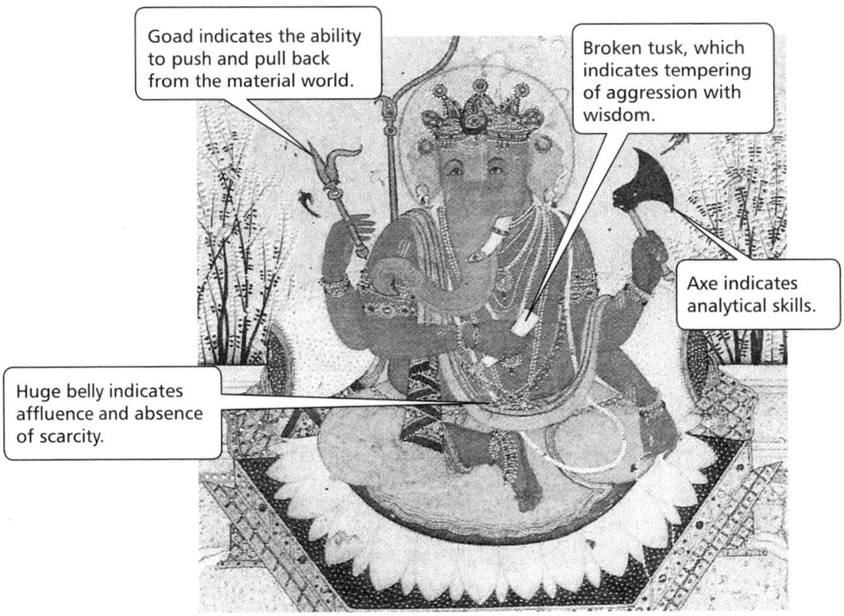

North Indian miniature of Ganesha

to bloom is the thousand-petalled lotus on top of the head. The first chakra that blooms is the Muladhara Chakra, located at the base of the spine near the anus. It marks the most basic instinct of man — the craving for food stemming from our fear of scarcity, and hence, death. Unless one outgrows this fear, the rise of the Kundalini and the journey to realisation of Shiva will not even begin. Only when Ganesha is realised will the journey begin.

Ganesha's wisdom manifests in the two symbols he carries in his hands. In one hand he holds an axe, and in the other hand he holds a noose. The axe represents analytical skills that enable one to separate objective from subjective reality, thought and form, animal instincts from human conditionings, sense of self from the sense of other, me from mine. The noose represents the ability to outgrow these divides, to unite the opposites, synthesise solutions, to recognise that ultimately, in nirguna brahman, Shiva and Shakti are not separate but one.

In some images, Ganesha holds a sugar cane in one hand and the elephant goad or ankush in the other. Sugar cane represents Kama, the god of desire and freedom. The elephant goad represents Yama, the god of death and bondage. Ganesha thus acknowledges the life-giving aspect of nature as well as the life-taking aspect of nature.

The lore of Shiva constantly refers to beheadings by Shiva. Shiva beheads Brahma. Shiva beheads Daksha. Shiva beheads Vinayaka. Each time the beheading is prompted by territorial behaviour resulting from amplified fear. But in Vinayaka's case, Shiva makes an error. Vinayaka is not being territorial. He is ignorant. He does

Bengali image of Parvati as Durga and her children

not know about Shiva, because Shiva has not contributed to his birth. Shiva is thus responsible for creating Vinayaka who ends up becoming his own obstacle. A restless Goddess may dance to arouse Shiva, but Shiva also has to dance to calm the Goddess. It is not a one-way street. It is in the human imagination that Purusha and Prakriti can move towards each other and finally meet. Ganesha embodies that possibility.

The Goddess can provide food to allay hunger. But Shiva has to give meaning to both food and hunger. Humans are the only creatures on earth, who can reflect on life. Humans wonder what is the purpose of life, why do we live, why do we eat. Nature offers no answer. Humans are able to domesticate the earth, establish fields and orchards and gardens and grow abundant food. Surrounded by great wealth, only humans wonder why do they have such power over nature. Humans can build great walls and establish rules and make themselves secure. But the heaviest of security does not take away death. Humans feel invalidated, weak and helpless, and wonder what is the point of human life. When no answer is forthcoming, a frightened man starts hoarding things, not just to secure his future, but to create the delusion of immortality. Our wealth and family, our possessions become an extension of our bodies. It is the fourth body – property that outlives the death of the other three. We hoard more and more property and thereby give ourselves meaning.

Yakshas are hoarders. They are visualised as enormously fat creatures who hoard wealth. They are closely associated with another race, also described as Rakshasas. Both share a common grandfather, Pulatsya, son of Brahma. It was Kubera, the leader of Yakshas, who built the golden city of Lanka. Ravana, leader

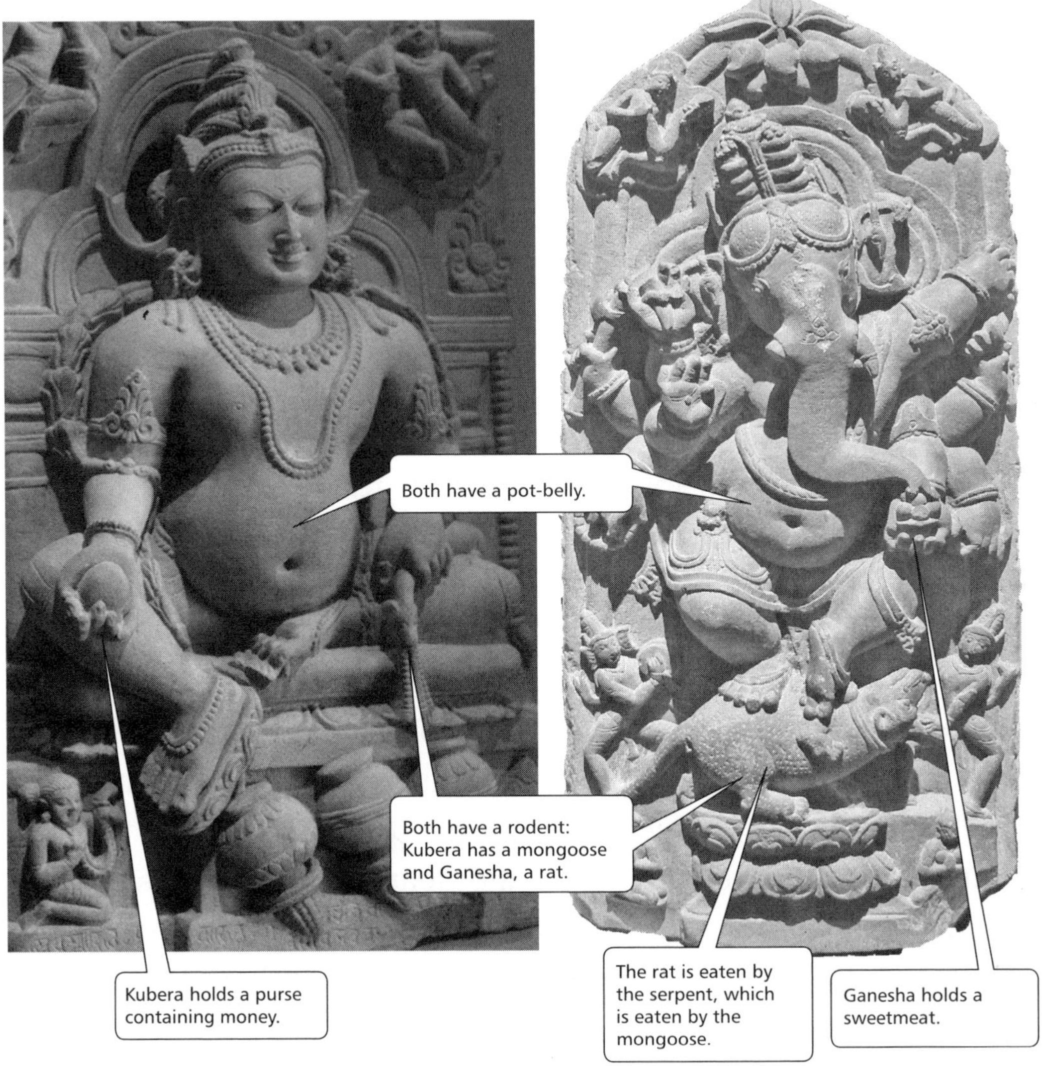

Stone images of Kubera and Ganesha

of Rakshasas, became jealous of Kubera. He drove Kubera out of Lanka and usurped the kingdom of Yakshas. Yakshas are thus creatures who have lost their home. No one gives them refuge, as everyone hates them. Everyone wants their treasures, not them. Abandoned and excluded by everyone they find refuge with Shiva. They become his Ganas.

Kubera keeps talking about all his wealth. So Parvati, who sits on Shiva's lap, reaches out, plucks out his left eye and eats it. Kubera howls in agony. 'Surely you can replace that eye with all your wealth,' says the Goddess. Kubera realises he cannot. He becomes aware of his mortality. He realises how wealth cannot compensate for his fear of death. Wealth cannot give meaning to existence. To remind himself of this, he replaces his lost eye with an eye of gold, which is why Kubera is called Pingalaksha, he with a golden eye. Shiva makes him the guardian of the northern direction, so that he will guide people towards wisdom.

Once, Kubera felt sorry for Ganesha. 'Let me feed you,' said Kubera, 'as clearly your father cannot afford to do so. You clearly look like someone who enjoys food.' Ganesha accepted Kubera's invitation, went to his house, and ate all that was offered. 'I am still hungry,' said the elephant-headed god. Kubera had to procure more food using the money in his treasury. Ganesha ate all that was served and kept asking for more. Finally Kubera fell at his feet and begged him to stop eating. 'You are draining my treasury dry,' he cried. Ganesha then said with a smile, 'You seek food to conquer hunger and end up hoarding food. My father shows how to outgrow hunger, and hence is happy even in the absence of food.'

Kubera and Ganesha are very similar to each other, yet very different. Kubera is a Gana but Ganesha is their leader. Kubera

Poster art of Ganesha with his father

Image of the sweetmeat modaka with dhurva grass

is Shiva's follower but Ganesha is Shiva's son. Kubera holds a money bag in his hand while Ganesha holds a moneybag-shaped sweetmeat called modaka in his hand. All living creatures need food to survive; humans hoard food to allay imaginary fears of future starvation. From this desire to hoard comes the notion of wealth and the craving for property and gold. Kubera indulges this hunger of man. Ganesha focuses on what really matters – food!

In nature, rats eat grain, snakes eat rats and mongooses eat snakes. Thus the mongoose is on top of the food chain. Kubera has the mongoose as his pet. Ganesha has the serpent around his belly and the rat at his feet. The predator and the prey are thus in harmony. This represents the idea of heaven – a perfect world without fear. Kubera thus seeks a world where he is the dominant overlord, while Ganesha symbolises a world where there is no need for a pecking order.

Kubera, the Gana, is trapped in the fear of scarcity and predation despite having wealth. That is why he hoards treasures but loses it all to the Rakshasas. Shiva makes Ganesha the leader of Ganas to help outgrow all fears. Only when fear is outgrown will the habit of hoarding be overcome. Only then will the Yakshas who came to Kailasa from Lanka truly discover the north, the land of the Pole Star, which represents a state of mind where there is no dependence on nature, no fear of death, no fear of scarcity or predation, only bliss.

The Rakshasas, like the Yakshas, are consumed by fear. That is why Ravana grabs what the Yakshas create. But that is not enough

Statue of Ravana and the cowherd

Poster art of Ganesha and Shiva

for Ravana. When he learns Kubera has now earned the affection of Shiva, he starts craving it as well. But rather than moving north towards Shiva, he seeks to bring Shiva south.

Shiva gives Ravana a Shiva-linga, instructing him not to place it on the ground before he reaches Lanka. The gods know that once the Shiva-linga reaches Lanka, the Rakshasa-king will never share him with the world. They beg Ganesha to stop Ravana. So Ganesha causes Ravana to experience an intense desire to answer the call of nature. He then takes the form of a boy and offers to hold the Shiva-linga while Ravana relieves himself. As soon as Ravana gives Ganesha the Shiva-linga and turns his back, Ganesha places the Shiva-linga on the ground. There it stands steadfast. No matter how much Ravana tries, it remains rooted to the spot. This Shiva-linga that Ganesha prevented from reaching Lanka is located at Gokarna, along the Konkan coast. Ganesha thus prevents the hoarding of Shiva by the Rakshasa-king.

In a similar story, Ravana's brother Vibhishana tries to take the image of Vishnu to Lanka. Once again, Ganesha foils this plan by placing the image of Vishnu on the ground while Vibhishana is performing his ablutions. This image of Vishnu known as Ranganatha is found on the banks of the river Kaveri. Ganesha is thus the obstacle to the hoarding of all things.

Ravana and Vibhishana look at divinity as commodities to be hoarded, which is why they seek to take Shiva and Vishnu to the south. They want divinity all for themselves. Like the hoarding Yakshas, they are not concerned about the other. This self-absorption is the consequence of fear. They want to secure themselves at the cost of the other. They are still pashu despite being surrounded by immense wealth and despite being in the presence of Shiva.

Calendar art showing Ganesha with his two wives, Riddhi and Siddhi

Ganesha therefore stops their journey south and forces them to look north, towards his father, towards wisdom.

That Shiva gives his son an elephant head is significant. Animals never overeat. Humans, because of imagined and amplified fears, end up spending their lives gathering food like the Yakshas and forget to reflect on the meaning of food. By replacing the human head with an elephant head, Shiva draws attention to human greed that is rooted in fear and that prevents humanity from discovering bliss. With the head of an animal that knows neither scarcity nor predator, Ganesha becomes the symbol of contentment and wisdom. His corpulent form evokes not just power and abundance but also satisfaction.

The elephant whose head is given to Ganesha is no ordinary elephant — it is found by Shiva's Ganas when they move in the northern direction as directed by Shiva. North is the direction associated with the Pole Star, with stillness, hence spiritual wisdom. The elephant is a symbol of material abundance. The elephant found in the north combines both ideas, and so is a befitting head for the son of Shiva and Shakti.

All the Ganas, including the Yakshas, accept Vinayaka as Ganesha, their leader. He makes them reflect on hoarding and inspires them towards contentment. The wives of Kubera, Riddhi and Nidhi, are associated with material growth and wealth accumulation, whereas Ganesha's two wives, Riddhi and Siddhi (sometimes called Buddhi), balance wealth with wisdom. Siddhi means emotional and intellectual maturity.

In calendar art, Ganesha is shown with Lakshmi instead of

Calendar art showing Ganesha with Lakshmi and Saraswati

Riddhi, and Saraswati instead of Siddhi. The two goddesses, draped in red and white, are associated with wealth and knowledge. If Lakshmi brings wealth, then Saraswati brings peace. The two are rarely seen together. Only Ganesha is able to bring them together. He removes the obstacle to wisdom.

Ganesha is said to have two sons, Shubh and Labh, which means 'auspiciousness' and 'profit'. His daughter is called Santoshi, goddess of satisfaction. These are metaphors to indicate that when Ganesha is brought into the house, he removes all obstacles to wealth, peace, auspiciousness, growth and happiness. He does so by enabling the potbellied Ganas to outgrow fear of scarcity. That is why he is their leader. That is why he is Ganapati.

6. Murugan's Secret

Face fear to outgrow it

Mysore painting of the boyish Murugan

Mysore painting of the six-headed Murugan

The Devas are not afraid of dying. They have Amrita, nectar of immortality. But fear of predation envelops them. Asuras are the predators, eyeing the good life of the Devas with hunger. It is for protection from the predatory Asura that the Devas wanted Shiva to marry. This story comes to us from the *Shiva Purana*, the *Skanda Purana* and the famous Sanskrit work *Kumara-Sambhava,* or the conception of Kumara, by the acclaimed poet, Kalidasa.

Kumara is the name of Shiva's other son. In some texts, Kumara is the elder son of Shiva and Parvati, while in other texts, he is younger, and Ganesha is the elder son. This difference is attributed to the fact that both Ganesha and Kumara are deities who became part of mainstream Hinduism much later in history.

While the worship of Ganesha received maximum attention in Maharashtra, the worship of Kumara is most popular in Tamil Nadu where he is known as Murugan. In all probability, he was originally a deity of southern hill tribes. While in the north, Kumara was feared and revered as a warrior-god, in the south Murugan was much admired and adored as a child, lover and guardian.

The story goes that there was an Asura called Taraka who had defeated the Devas and overrun their paradise. The only way to restore cosmic balance was by killing him. But Taraka had a boon: only a little baby who led an army could kill him. The Devas wondered how they could produce a warrior who was strong and mature enough to fight a battle even though he was a baby. They approached their father, Brahma, who informed them that such

Clay dolls of Shiva's two sons

a child that defies the law of nature can be produced by Purusha alone. In other words, Shiva.

In Tantrik physiology, a child is born when the white seed of man merges with the red seed of woman. From the father, a child gets the nervous tissue, including the brain, which enables humans to imagine and access spiritual reality. From the mother, the child gets flesh and blood. In other words, the father is the source of Purusha and the mother, the source of Prakriti. Ganesha is the mother's child, a child of Prakriti. Now the gods want the father's child, a child of Purusha.

In mythology, a man can produce a child outside a woman's womb if the white seed is adequately energised by the spiritual fire, tapas. That is why Tapasvins are able to create children without the intervention of women. Rishi Bharadvaja is able to father Drona when, on seeing a nymph, he sheds his semen in a pot. Rishi Vyasa is able to father Suka when, on catching sight of a nymph, he sheds his semen on fire sticks. Rishi Vibhandak is able to father Rishyashringa through a doe that eats his semen, shed at the sight of a beautiful woman. Devas realise that to kill Taraka they need semen that has not been shed for eons. It must be so powerful that it can germinate into a child without needing any womb to incubate it. Such white seed, they learn from Brahma, exists only in the body of Shiva.

To get Shiva to release the seed, the gods first sent Kama, the god of lust. But he fails miserably, and is reduced to ashes by a glance of Shiva's third eye. So the gods appeal to Shakti, the Goddess herself, to do the needful.

As Parvati, daughter of the mountains, Shakti prays to Shiva, appeals to his compassion, and secures him as a husband. She

Chola bronze of Shiva, Parvati and Kartikeya

forces him to acknowledge her. In Tantrik narratives, she sits on top of him and serves as his teacher and guide. But despite this, Shiva refuses to shed his seed. Metaphorically speaking, he is engaged with the world through his lovemaking but is still detached. The world stimulates him but he is not ensnared by it.

In the Puranas, when Indra, king of the Devas, feels that a Tapasvin will use his tapa to dethrone him, he sends an Apsara to seduce the Tapasvin. Tapasvins are fire-ascetics (tapa = fire) and Apsaras are water-nymphs (apsa = water). They compete. She tries to enchant him while he resists her charms. Sometimes, the Tapasvin succeeds and the Apsara leaves him alone. Sometimes, the Apsara succeeds and the Tapasvin sheds his semen, fathers a child, and loses all the power he gained through tapasya, much to Indra's satisfaction. Shiva, however, refuses to shed his seed, despite the intervention of Kama. So on behalf of the Devas, the Goddess appeals to Shiva to shed his seed.

The Devas have another problem. They cannot let Shiva's semen enter Shakti's womb and have a child produced the normal way. For Shakti's red seed is equal in power to Shiva's white seed. They will neutralise each other and create a powerful, but normal, child. They want the child to be hyper-masculine, capable of fighting battle even when he is barely six days old. They do not want him to possess anything feminine in him. Once again, this is a metaphor.

The Devas do not want a child of nature, who like all living creatures, suffers from the fear of scarcity and predators. They want a child who suffers no such fears. Shiva has no such fears, but is totally detached from the world. The Devas want a child who is like Shiva in all respects, except that he actively engages with the world, protects against all predators and provides sanctuary to the

North Indian warrior-god Kumara

Temple wall image showing Kartikeya ready to launch an assault prey. He will be celibate but not innocent, ignorant or gullible. He will be Kumara, the wise and capable boy-god.

Early narratives describe how the Devas enter the caves of Kailasa, interrupt the lovemaking of Shiva, embarrass Shakti who moves away, enabling Agni, the fire-god, to claim Shiva's semen, which is why Kumara is also called Skanda, the spurt of life. In later narratives, on the request of Shakti and the Devas, Shiva releases his power in the form of six fiery sparks and hands them over to Agni.

Seed or sparks, they are so hot and potent, that even the fire-god cannot withstand their heat. He gives them to Vayu, the wind-god. Even Vayu is unable to cool them down. Vayu gives them to Ganga. The water of the river-goddess starts to boil. The Sara-vana, or forest of reeds, on the banks of the Ganga bursts into flames because of the heat. When the fire dies out, in the embers are found six children. They cry for their mother. The six Pleiades, or the stars of the Kritika constellation, nurse the six babies. Finally Shakti holds the six children in her arms and turns them into a single child with six heads, and finally a child with one head. The first thing the child asks for is a weapon. Shakti gives him the vel, or spear. Thus is born Vel Murugan, the spear-bearing warrior god, ready to do battle on the seventh day of his life.

The Kritikas, or the six stars of the Pleiades constellation, play a key role in the story of Murugan. The Great Bear Constellation is composed of seven stars associated with seven sages known as the Sapta Rishis. Each of them had a wife. One day the seven women were bathing in a pond in which the Devas had placed the

Festival idol of Kartikeya in Bengal

Festival idol of Kartikeshwara in Odisha

six sparks of Shiva, and this made six of the seven wives pregnant. The Rishis accused them of adultery and threw them out of the house. The six wives rejected the children in their wombs and became the Pleiades constellation, or the Kritika Nakshatra. The six discarded foetuses set the forest of reeds aflame, and from the fire emerged Murugan. The sight of Murugan angers the Kritikas who try to harm him at first, but the child's cherubic charm calms them down. Murugan understands their plight and declares that whosoever does not worship them and acknowledge them as his mothers would suffer greatly. Murugan transforms the Kritika maids into wild, fearsome goddesses known as the Matrikas, who live in the forest, and can cause children to suffer fatal fevers with pox and rashes, unless they are venerated. Murugan, the son of the Kritikas, is known as Kartikeya.

As the son of Agni, Murugan is known as Agneya. As the son of Vayu, he is known as Guha, the mysterious one. As the son of the forest of reeds, he is known as Saravana. As the six-headed one, he is known as Shanmughan or Aramughan. As the wild red-coloured warrior, he is Senthil. As the warrior who looks like a baby, he is called Kumara.

On the seventh day of his life, Murugan stepped into battle. He fought and killed Taraka with the spear his mother gave him.

In the *Skanda Purana*, which is a Tamil scripture extolling the tales of Murugan, the story does not end with the death of Taraka. Taraka's two brothers, Simhamukhan and Surpadman, continue the battle. After a fierce battle, Murugan defeats Simhamukhan. Simhamukhan begs for mercy and promises to serve him in any way if his life is spared. Murugan then tells Simhamukhan to serve his mother, Shakti, as her vahana, or mount. Simhamukhan turns

Stone carving of Shakti with her two sons, Ganesha and Kartikeya into the lion that Shakti rides when she transforms into Durga.

The battle with Surpadman is the fiercest of all. Finally Surpadman turns into a gigantic mountain in an attempt to withstand Murugan's onslaught. Murugan hurls his spear and splits the mountain in two. One half turns into a rooster. The other half turns into a peacock. The rooster becomes Murugan's emblem and the peacock becomes his vehicle.

Murugan thus defeats the enemies of the Devas and is declared the commander of all celestial armies. Through him, Shiva becomes the guardian of the Devas.

Murugan is visualised as a muscular god surrounded by symbols of martial power and authority such as a spear, a peacock and a rooster. Ganesha, in contrast, has a corpulent body and a potbelly and is associated with symbols of fertility such as grass, rat and serpent. Murugan is the warrior son of the Goddess, while Ganesha is the scholar son. Murugan is renowned for killing demons, while Ganesha is renowned for his cleverness.

Of course, this is not entirely true. In Maharashtra, where Ganesha is the most popular deity, there are legends of how he killed many demons. And in Tamil Nadu, where Murugan is most worshipped, there are stories of how he revealed the secret of the sacred sound, Om, to his father, Shiva. Thus the two brothers compete with each other in matters of brain and brawn. Through them, the distant Shiva reaches out to the common man, much like how Vishnu reaches out through his many avatars.

Narada, the wily, trouble-making sage, once wanted to know which of Shiva's two sons could go fastest around the world

Poster art of Ganesha and Kartikeya on a race

three times. Murugan leapt onto his peacock and flew around the world three times but was declared the loser because his brother, Ganesha, had simply gone around his parents three times and said, 'I went around my emotional world, which matters more than the external world that my brother went around.' Murugan argued his case but the decision had been taken. Furious, Murugan left his father's house and went south of the Vindhyas.

Murugan's movement to the south is metaphorical as well as real. North is the realm of Shiva; the realm of stillness and wisdom. South is the realm of Shakti; the realm of movement and fear. The Goddess moves north to turn Shiva into Shankara. Their son now returns to the south, to help humanity outgrow every fear.

In the geographical north, Murugan is the ascetic-warrior who fights wars where men die and women become widows. But in the south, Murugan is the wise and responsible householder-guardian with many wives, who fights demons while his mother, Kotravai, a local name for Kali, drinks the blood of the fallen.

Murugan embodies Shiva's wisdom expressed when Shiva takes the form of Dakshinamurti, the teacher who faces south. Knowing Shiva to be Adi-nath, or the primal teacher, all the sages rushed north towards the Himalayas to hear Shiva's discourse. This rush to the north created a cosmic imbalance. The earth began to tilt north. Sensing trouble, Shiva asked his foremost disciple and devotee, the Rishi Agastya, to move south with his students, until the end of the discourse.

As Agastya moved south, the sun-god, Surya, sought his help. He said that the Vindhya mountain that separated the north from

Stone image of Agastya

Poster art of the Siddhas

the south was growing in size and blocking his path. 'Please stop his growth so that I can travel the sky without any obstacle.' Agastya promised to help. On seeing Agastya, the Vindhya mountain bowed in reverence. 'If you truly respect me,' said the Rishi, 'then stay in this bent position until I return north.' Vindhya agreed. To ensure that the mountain never rose again, Agastya remained in the south. There, he spread his wisdom through students who were known as the Siddhas, because Agastya taught them the siddhis or the secrets of alchemy. Agastya also composed the Tamil language.

Agastya is said to have brought the river Kaveri to the south. Ganesha, in the form of a crow, toppled Agastya's water pot, which contained the water of the Ganga, and so was born the river Kaveri, on whose banks flourished the Tamil culture.

Agastya missed the northern Himalayas so much that Shiva asked one of his Ganas, Idumba, to carry two mountain peaks south. The names of the two peaks were Shiva-giri and Shakti-giri. Idumba carried the two mountain peaks in a kavadi, a bamboo pole slung over the shoulder, with each peak hanging on either end in baskets. It was a long and tiring journey. At one point, after crossing the Vindhyas, Idumba placed the mountains on the ground and rested. When he tried picking up the kavadi again, he could not. One of the peaks had become too heavy. He noticed a young boy seated on it, pushing the mountain down. He realised this was no ordinary boy; it had to be a son of Shiva. Idumba bowed to the lad, who identified himself as Murugan and made the hill his home. Today, that hill is known as Palani and is one of the sacred spots for devotees of Murugan.

In Tamil Nadu, devotees of Murugan often carry a kavadi which is decorated with peacock feathers. A similar practice is seen in

Kavadi carried by Murugan-worshippers in the south

Kanwariyas, who carry the holy water of the Ganges on a sling north India where devotees of Shiva, the Kanwariyas, carry pots of Ganga water. The kavadi is a symbol of worldly responsibilities that entrap humans in the material world. Murugan moves to the metaphorical south to help his devotees fulfil their responsibilities and to remind them that they have not been abandoned by Shiva.

Across India there are many ascetics who shun the householder's life but are guardians of village communities. Murugan is the most famous one. And like Murugan, other guardian gods are identified either as local manifestations of Shiva or his sons.

In Tulsidas's *Ram Charit Manas*, which is a retelling of the Ramayana written in the 15th century in north India, Hanuman, the monkey-god who helps Ram defeat the Rakshasa-king Ravana, is called an avatar of Shiva.

In Tamil Nadu is another village god known as Aiyanar, who is born when the seed of Shiva is incubated in the womb of six Matrikas. He is shown riding an elephant or a horse. Sometimes, he has a dog next to him. He is a village guardian god, to whom villagers offer votive terracotta horses.

There are stories of how Shiva shed semen when he saw Mohini, the female form of Vishnu. From the shed semen were born the various warrior-gods who protect the villages of India, Hanuman included.

In Kerala, the son of Shiva and Mohini is called Ayyappa or Manikantha. He is Hari-Hara-Suta, the son of Hari (Vishnu) and Hara (Shiva). He is raised by the local king who has no children of his own. When the queen bears a son of her own, she becomes insecure and tries to harm Ayyappa. She asks him to fetch for her

Poster art of Hanuman

Poster art of Ayyappa

Aiyanar, the village god of Tamil Nadu with his companions

the milk of a tigress, hoping that the quest will result in his death. Instead, the boy goes to the forest, encounters and kills a demoness called Mahishi, finds a tigress, milks her, and returns to the city riding a tiger. This reveals his divinity, and the queen realises her mistake. She begs for forgiveness. Ayyappa declares that he will never marry; he gives the kingdom to the queen's son and promises to be the guardian of the kingdom from atop a nearby hill.

Like Murugan, Ayyappa stands on a hill. He is a very masculine god who shuns female company. So does Hanuman, who serves Ram. Celibacy and ascetic practices are closely associated with Shiva. It indicates nivritti-marga, withdrawal from the world. Serving as a warrior, however, indicates participation in worldly affairs. It indicates interest in worldly matters. Celibate warrior sons of Shiva thus embody that aspect of Shiva which is more connected with culture. Through these forms, Shiva acknowledges the human yearning for sanctuary and security.

The city of Kashi is associated with Kotwals, or policemen, who are called Bhairavas. In this form, Shiva protects the town like a guard dog. He is feared and appeased by travellers who seek entry into the city. Without his permission, no one can enter. This role of doorkeeper and guardian is often performed by gods who are both celibate and warriors. Goddess temples are flanked by images of two Bhairavas, the white Bhairava and the black Bhairava, locally known as Gora Bhairo and Kala Bhairo. Shiva here plays a very mundane, earthy role. There is nothing transcendent in this function. In Ram temples, Hanuman plays the role of guardian and doorkeeper.

In the Deccan region, there is Khandoba, or Mallana, a warrior-god who rides a white stallion and goes into battle with his

Poster art of Khandoba, the guardian-god from Maharashtra

dog. He fights the demons Mani and Malla, and secures the land for the local villagers. He is visualised with a thick moustache and glaring eyes, visuals that are aimed to enhance his machismo. He was the patron god of the Maratha warriors who controlled India in the 17th century. Like a warlord, he is associated with horses and dogs. He came to be identified with the more aggressive and martial forms of Shiva: Virabhadra, the righteous warrior, and Bhairava, the fearsome warrior.

Khandoba is, however, married. He has many wives. And these wives are daughters of local village communities. One of his wives belongs to the shepherd community. Another belongs to the trading community. Another is the daughter of a tailor and a fourth is the daughter of a gardener. Other wives belong to communities of oil pressers, even Muslims. Thus through marriage, Khandoba, the guardian god of the village, is anchored to the village community. He protects them and they give him wives for pleasure.

There is great dispute in the scriptures about whether Murugan is married or single. In north India, he is typically seen as a lone bachelor god who is obsessed with war; women shun his shrine. In south India, he is typically seen with two wives, Valli and Sena. Marriage is a metaphor for worldliness.

According to one tale, after killing Taraka, Kartikeya was so filled with energy and passion that he yearned the company of women. But the women did not want his company as he was the god of war and full of bloodlust. Wherever he went he brought destruction and death. Every time Kartikeya approached a woman, they appeared to him either as his mother or as mourning

Poster art of Murugan, the boy-god

widows. This is why Kartikeya never got married and that is why in the few north Indian temples of Kartikeya, women choose to stay out.

In Haryana, in Pahowa, Kurukshetra district, is a temple dedicated to Kartikeya. No woman is allowed to enter this temple as the deity here is a bachelor and because the deity is the god of war and death. The deity, identified with Kartikeya, has no skin. He gave it to his mother so that no woman would find him attractive and so not marry him and risk becoming a war widow. Oil is poured on the body of this war-mongering deity to calm him down and to please all soldiers who have died in battle. It is said that Yudhishtira was advised by Krishna to visit this shrine and pour oil on the image of Kartikeya after the Mahabharata war, in which eighteen million warriors were killed, so as to seek the forgiveness of the dead.

According to another tale, Kartikeya was upset when his parents chose to give Ganesha wives first. Feeling that his mother favoured Ganesha over him, Kartikeya left his northern abode and moved south.

The southern direction is associated with Yama, with death, with change, with fear. Shakti came from the south. In the south lives Daksha, her father, who through yagna domesticates nature and creates culture. Shiva holds culture in disdain, but his son goes south and assimilates his father's ascetic wisdom with the ways of culture. This is metaphorically expressed through marriage.

Murugan marries twice. The first marriage is an arranged marriage, an expression of social obligation. This wife is Devasena,

Gigantic image of the bachelor Murugan from the Batu caves, Malaysia

Rare temple of Kartikeya in north India at Pahowa, Kurukshetra, Haryana

Image of Murugan with two wives from a Tamil temple shrine

or Sena. She is the daughter of Indra given to Murugan in gratitude for defeating Taraka. Devasena means 'army of the gods', and so can also be seen as the embodiment of a thought: Murugan is married to his army.

The second marriage is the result of romance and passion. The woman who wins Murugan's ascetic heart with her raw tribal energy is Valli. She was found by her father, Nampi, a tribal chief, in a hole dug by women looking for wild forest yams (valli), hence her name. She is thus a child of the forest. When she comes of age, she is asked to guard her father's millet field. And that is when Murugan hears of her from the sage Narada, who is instrumental in bringing him to the south.

Murugan comes down from his hill and is smitten by this young girl. He takes the form of a young warrior and woos her. She hesitates. She is not sure how to respond. Suddenly a wild elephant appears and a frightened Valli seeks refuge in Murugan's arms. The elephant turns out to be Ganesha who removes all obstacles. Valli succumbs to Murugan's charm. She is besotted by his power. She surrenders to his will.

Songs and stories describe the love of Murugan and Valli. How she keeps it a secret from her father, how everyone in the village notices the sorrow of the girl when she is not in the millet field, the secret trysts a female companion orchestrates between the lovers. The mood is passionate, romantic and clandestine. At first Murugan is unable to understand Valli's apprehension. As the son of a hermit and as the warlord of the gods, he is not familiar with the ways of culture and the concerns of a father for a daughter. Finally, he understands and presents himself in full splendour to Nampi. Nampi realises that his daughter's secret

Murugan with Valli and Sena

lover is none other than the patron deity of his tribe, the warrior-god who lives atop a hill. He bows to Murugan and welcomes him home as son-in-law.

Thus while Ganesha helps devotees move from south to north, Kartikeya himself moves from north to south for the benefit of devotees. While Ganesha tempers materialistic cravings with spiritual insight, Murugan tempers his martial attitude with divine grace and romantic emotions. Thus the Goddess helps Shiva connect with humanity through her two sons.

7. Nataraja's Secret

Destruction is deconstruction

Modern sculpture of Shiva as the lone ascetic

Image from Maharashtra showing Shiva as Shankara, the householder

Brahma creates. Shiva destroys. Brahma is not worshipped. Shiva is worshipped. This is because Brahma creates Kama, Yama, and Tripura — desire, death and three worlds. Shiva is Kamantaka, Yamantaka and Tripurantaka — destroyer of desire, death and the three worlds.

Humans desire life, fear death and construct three worlds because humans fear death more than any other living creature on earth. Our fear is greater because we can imagine. We imagine what happens after death, we imagine a world without death, we imagine a world without us and wonder what is the point of life. Unable to make sense of things, we try to control life — we get attached to things, we resist change and we create property. Human civilisation is thus rooted in fear. It is a delusion. Brahmanda or culture is maya.

The first people who brought the word 'maya' into English were 18th-century scholars who lived when Europe was in the throes of the scientific revolution. They used the word 'illusion' to translate the word 'maya', and the word 'destroyer' to describe Shiva. Since Hindus describe the world as maya and worship Shiva, Europeans concluded that Hindus were a people who held worldly life in disdain. This romantic, exotic, world-denying perception of India, in general, and Hinduism, in particular, still persists as tourist brochures are full of images of the Kumbha Mela at Allahabad, where naked mendicants smeared with ash and holding tridents, just like Shiva, line up to bathe at the confluence of the Ganga and Yamuna every twelve years.

The European gaze was assumed to be scientific, objective, free of bias and hence modern. However, in the 1970s, scholars realised

Poster art of Shiva as the householder

Miniature painting of Shiva as the householder

that 'modern' thought was actually not as logical and free of bias as it was claimed to be; it was informed by cultural prejudices. The translations of European scholars were clearly based on the one-life framework. Since the God of the Bible is described as creator and hence worthy of worship, they were bewildered as to why Hindus worship Shiva, not Brahma, a conundrum that still persists in modern academia. This was postmodern thinking. Hindu ideas need to be seen in the Hindu context, not using the one-life framework of Europeans, but the rebirth framework of Indians. When this is done, a more appropriate translation of maya is 'construction'. Shiva then does not destroy; he deconstructs!

The word 'construction' emerged as part of the postmodern vocabulary; it was not part of the modern (or rather pre postmodern) vocabulary of the 18th century. Thus 18th century scholars were ill-equipped to explain Indian thoughts.

Construction means a perception of the world shaped by a measuring scale that depends on cultural norms and personal prejudices. This perception changes every time there is a change in cultural norms and/or personal prejudices. What is considered right or good or beautiful today may not be considered so tomorrow, all sensory inputs remaining the same. Thus the perception can be 'de-constructed' and 're-constructed'. The word 'illusion' came from typical scientific arrogance that logic can decipher the truth free of all bias. The word 'construction' admits that all understanding is rooted in bias.

For Hindus, maya is a constructed reality. More accurately, maya is the measuring scale that values and devalues all things in Prakriti, and by doing so gives rise to Brahmanda, an individual's perception of the world. It is neither a bad thing nor is it a good

Image of Shiva as the formless linga

thing. It is just the way the human mind perceives reality. Animals do not live in maya, because they do not possess imagination. Human beings do. Humans are therefore subject to maya.

The intention of tapasya is to reflect on and deconstruct and be liberated from it. Tapa or spiritual fire burns maya and destroys Brahmanda. Shiva, the lord of Tapasvins, is therefore the destroyer of maya. Maya nurtures aham, the ego, that imagines itself to be master of the world. Shiva destroys aham so that atma or soul can be realised. When this happens, human life is validated. Pashu, or animal, becomes Purusha.

When there is no construction, when there is no maya, when there is no perceived reality, no aham, what remains is the linga, the pillar of Shiva. This is possible only when the human imagination has no fear. The absence of fear fills the mind with bliss. This is ananda. This is the linga, the erect phallus of Shiva. It is Swayambhu, self-created and self-contained, as it does not depend on external stimuli for its existence. This can only happen when there is wisdom. But wisdom for whom?

Humans are the only creatures who can imagine other people's fear. Humans can empathise. The Shiva-linga therefore does not stand alone; encasing it is the Shakti-yoni, the womb of the Goddess. She is the temple in which the linga is enshrined. She is the world around the temple. She is the water pot hanging above the Shiva-linga, dripping water on him, making sure he does not shut his eyes, but opens them to look at the other. Shakti thus ensures Shiva looks at jiva, humanity that has succumbed to aham, maya and Brahmanda out of fear.

Shiva as Dakshinamurti, the teacher

It is ironical that Shiva, the hermit-god of Hinduism, is the only Hindu god to be visualised as a householder with a wife and children. All gods have a consort by their side — Vishnu has Lakshmi, Ram has Sita, Krishna has Radha — but no one is visualised with their children apart from Shiva.

Shakti is nature. In nature, all creatures fear death. That is why they hunt for food and are wary of predators. Through Ganesha, Shakti makes Shiva take away fear of scarcity. Through Kartikeya, Shakti makes Shiva take away fear of the predator. With these two fears gone, humanity can focus on its greatest fear — the fear of meaninglessness, the fear of invalidation. It can resist the creation of aham, and realise the atma.

To facilitate this deconstruction, Shiva becomes the primal teacher, Adi-nath. Adi-nath teaches the world in two forms, either as Dakshinamurti or as Nataraja.

Dakshinamurti means the one who sits facing south. In this form, Shiva sits under the still Pole Star in the shade of the banyan tree. Nothing moves here, nothing grows here, except wisdom. Here, sages sit at Shiva's feet in rapt attention.

The direction that Shiva faces is the direction of Yama, of death, of change. Shiva helps his students face this change with wisdom. He draws attention to the three forms of change: natural, social and personal. Animals experience only one kind of change — the natural, the change of seasons and tides. Communities experience changing values of society. Social values change as one moves from place to place; and social values in one place invariably change over time. In addition, individuals experience personal change,

Stone carving of dancing Shiva from Badami, Karnataka

The three blades of a trident and three leaves of a bilva sprig change that happens when context changes. We behave differently in times of prosperity and differently in times of crisis. Our own understanding of the world changes as we experience fortune and misfortune.

The linga is offered the sprig of the bel or bilva, which has three leaves joined at the stem. The three leaves represent the three changes: of nature or Prakriti, of society or Sanskriti and of individual perception of Brahmanda. The stem is wisdom that we seek from the teacher, the wisdom that will help us recognise maya, and appreciate the various constructions that shape our notions of reality.

The blades of Shiva's trident symbolise Tripura, the three constructions we occupy because of maya. It means the natural world, the cultural world and the personal world. It also means the world of 'me' (our physical and mental body), 'mine' (the wealth and knowledge and relationships we claim ownership over and control) and 'not mine' (all things we do not claim ownership over and are unable to control). It also means the three bodies: sthula sharira (physical body), sukshma sharira (conscious mind full of opinions) and karana sharira (unconscious mind full of impressions). The staff that Shiva holds is the staff of wisdom, the linga beyond the maya.

Shiva's sacred mark, the Tripundra, is made of three horizontal lines of ash. Ash means that which survives when matter is destroyed. Ash represents the atma that never dies. The three lines represent the three worlds that are deconstructed and destroyed by Shiva's third eye of wisdom.

Miniature of Shiva emerging from light

As Dakshinamurti, Shiva sits atop Kailasa, the heat of tapa locked in his body turning the world around him into a desolate snow-clad landscape. This Shiva is the impatient and angry Rudra who beheads Brahma and transforms into Kapalika. This Shiva is Bhairava with the dogs and Virabhadra with the sword. This Shiva is alone.

Shakti draws the heat out, causes the snow to melt and turn into the Ganga that flows down to fertilise the plains and sustain human settlements. On the banks of the Ganga, she invites Shiva to settle in her city, Kashi, as Shankar-Shambho, the kind, benevolent, understanding form of God.

Kashi is the city of Ganga and Gauri, known locally as Annapurna, the kitchen goddess. Ganga and Gauri are two aspects of Shakti, one representing the bubbly river and the other the patient mountain. The two goddesses make Shiva understand and empathise with human fears and frailties in Kashi. Here, the head of Brahma, which clings to Shiva's fingers and sears into his palm after being severed, is washed away at the Kapala-mochan-ghat, because Ganga forgives all crimes, even the vile, incestuous gaze of Brahma. Here, Shiva becomes the lovable Shambhu who is both the dog-riding Kala Bhairava, remover of malevolent spirits, and the bhang-drinking Gora Bhairava, who enjoys the company of ghosts. Here, he is Vishwa-nath, master of the world. Only in Kashi does the Ganga flow northward, drawn by the wisdom of Dakshinamurti.

Further south, in Chidambaram, he is the dancer, Nataraja. He teaches through dance because words are too literal to capture the essence of the intangible nirguna. One needs symbols that dance is best able to communicate. A book occupies space but not

South Indian painting of Shiva as Nataraja

Poster art of Shiva as Nataraja

time, a discourse occupies time but not space, a dance occupies both space and time. It can be seen and heard and read. It is a performance that appeals to the senses, stirs the emotions and demands intellectual analysis. In the process, tools to deconstruct maya are passed on.

The story goes that a group of Mimansikas was performing yagna in a forest when Shiva walked past naked. Shiva was totally oblivious to them for he was in a state of bliss. The Mimansikas, however, were distracted by him and held him responsible for the distraction.

Mimamsa means investigation or inquiry. Mimansikas are those who yearn to understand the meaning of life. Mimamsa is divided into two schools: the early school or Purva Mimamsa and later school or Uttar Mimamsa. This division emerged as the former school paid too much attention to form and failed to realise that thought had shaped the form. The later school paid great attention to the thought of the form.

Those who were performing the yagna saw Shiva's form and did not see the thought. What they saw frightened them. They saw a man who was so content and blissful, he did not need all the things the Mimansikas aspired for. He did not seek wealth, he did not seek knowledge, he did not seek power. He was self-assured, self-contained and self-fulfilled. The sight of the naked Shiva made them feel inadequate and insecure. He possessed what they did not possess. And they felt their wives would leave their sides and chase Shiva.

In fear, they saw Shiva as a predator and decided to destroy

South Indian bronze sculpture of Shiva as Urdhva-Nataraja

him. Using their knowledge of yagna, they invoked creatures from the fire and unleashed them against Shiva. First came the tiger, then a serpent, and finally a demon.

Shiva showed no signs of fear. He simply caught the tiger by its jaw, skinned it alive and wrapped its hide, dripping with blood, around his body. Shiva then picked up the snake and put it around his neck; there it sat, still, with upraised hood. Finally, Shiva jumped on the back of the demon, breaking his back, and started to dance, the only music being provided by his rattle-drum.

At first the Mimansikas were terrified. They realised this naked man was no ordinary man. Fear turned to awe as the performance continued; it was mesmerising! Shiva's hands, feet and body moved gracefully, in perfect coordination. His whole form seemed to expand. The ends of his hair rose up to touch the skies; the stars and the planets stopped to gaze. The tips of his fingers grazed the horizons where the gods assembled, spellbound. The thud of footsteps forced the demons and serpents to rise from their subterranean kingdoms. Such a performance had never been seen before. No nymph had danced like this. Shiva's consort, Shakti, smiled from afar as she fell in love once again.

The Rishi Bharata made a note of all that he saw: the change in expressions or abhinayas, the twists of the body known as angikas, the hand gestures known as mudras, the mood evoked known as bhavas, the feelings stirred known as rasas. All this he put down in the Natya-shastra, the treatise on the performing arts.

The Mimansikas realised this was no ordinary performance. Unlike a gentle, seductive dance which is meant to enchant, known as lasya, this was tandava, forceful, as if demanding attention and evoking thought. Shiva was communicating. This was not

Shiva dancing on one foot

entertainment. This was enlightenment. This was the Ananda-Tandava, the dance of bliss.

Shiva struck a whole series of poses in order to stir the imagination. He finally froze. This final pose contained the wisdom of the Vedas. What had not been realised by the Mimansikas after performing hundreds of rituals was realised by that one dance pose.

Shiva's right palm was upraised. This is the a-bhaya mudra or the gesture that communicates 'do not fear'. Shiva sensed the fear of the Mimansikas. Why were they so obsessed with the yagna? Because the ritual made them feel less afraid as it granted them control of the world around them.

To feel safe, the Mimansikas had created the Jyotisha-shastra, that enabled them to study the stars and planets and predict the future. They had created the Vastu-shastra that enabled them to control the movement of energies across eight directions, so that positive forces moved their way. They had put together Dhanur-vidya, that enabled them to create weapons and secure themselves. They even had Ayur-veda, the science of health and healing that offered the promise of immortality. But despite all this, fear still remained. Because the source of the fear had not been understood.

The upraised right palm is strategically placed on the left hand that is pointing to the left foot that swings across the right leg and is poised midair. Attention is thus being drawn to the moving left leg.

This raising of the left foot leaves the body imbalanced. Yet Shiva is balanced, calm and composed. He holds this position without

South Indian painting of Shiva Ekapada

thoughts of falling down. He is comfortable. He is Shiva Ekapada, the one who stands on one leg.

The left leg is in fact in motion; it moves round and round creating a ring. It represents the precariousness of existence, the endless change of nature, and the transformations of the world. The left leg thus mimics nature that is the source of fear.

That the left hand and the left leg are moving towards the right, makes one wonder what is so special about the right side. In mythic vocabulary, the left side of the body is associated with the rhythm of the material world because it is where the heart is located. Just as the heart beats at regular intervals, the material world goes through rhythmic changes in the form of tides and seasons. The right half then becomes the side of spiritual reality; it is still and silent. The left side represents Prakriti, nature's constant change. The right side is Purusha, the human potential to stay still. To exist, one needs both sides, left and right, Prakriti and Purusha.

The Mimansikas are unable to still their mind. Faced with the whirling material world, their mind goes into a spin. They use rituals to fight change, and fail. But still, they continue to fight back with more rituals as they know no better. Shiva presents an option, a way out from fear, not by controlling nature but by recognising the truth of nature.

The tiger killed fearlessly by Shiva represents nature that frightens Brahma. Shiva refuses to let nature intimidate him. At the same time, he does not seek to control or domesticate nature. He observes nature like the serpent coiled around his neck. The hooded cobra is

Stone sculpture from Belur, Karnataka, of dancing Shiva

the symbol of the alert and still Tapasvin who sits unmoving and watches with full attention the world around it.

Unlike the Mimansikas who were busy conducting rituals to tame nature, the Tapasvin observed the rhythms of Nature — manifesting as breath, heartbeat, tides and seasons. He also observed the rhythms of culture and the rhythms of thoughts and emotions in every human being. He saw how fortune follows misfortune, joy follows sorrow, excitement follows boredom, pain follows pleasure. On careful, focused attention, he realised that everything changes over time — some things change by the second, some by centuries, but all things material and tangible have to change form. The body has to age and die. Ideas come and go. Societies rise and fall. But new life is always being created. Thus nothing ends forever. There is always a new beginning.

This cyclical view of things is represented by the wheel of fire in which Shiva dances. It is the wheel known as samsara or the wheel of rebirth. All living creatures die and are reborn. All thoughts and dreams rise and fall. At each birth a different form is taken, sometimes human and sometimes animal. At death this body is discarded. Shiva advises the Mimansikas to sit back, sit still and observe this. Awareness will take away anxiety and fear. It will bring repose and faith.

Although nature's truth is timeless, we often forget it. Shiva dances on the back of a demon called Apasmara, which means the demon of forgetfulness. We forget that what goes around comes around. As we suffer the winter cold, we forget that the previous year it was cold too but it did pass. As we suffer, we imagine the suffering will never end. Apasmara makes Brahma forget who he really is, who he was before he chased Shatarupa, before he

Chola bronze of Shiva as Nataraja

sprouted five heads, before Shiva severed one of them. We humans forget what our mind was before it was contaminated by imagined, amplified fear. We forget that we construct Brahmanda, subjective reality, to cope with objective reality. We forget that only we can destroy this Brahmanda, with its three constituent worlds of 'me', 'mine' and 'not mine'. Because we have the third eye of wisdom.

When two people meet, initially fear governs the relationship. This fear goes away when each one is convinced the other is no threat. This fear is amplified when one dominates the other. Shiva offers the third way, one where fear is outgrown. This happens when one empathises with the other, when there is love for the other, when one recognises the autonomy of the other and neither seeks to dominate or be dominated or dependent in any way. But to empathise with the other, we have to look at the other, not in fear, but with genuine affection and sensitivity. This is darshan, the gaze of understanding.

Nataraja's two upper arms hold up the options that we have as we go through life. In one hand he holds the damaru, or rattle-drum, while in the other he holds tapa, the spiritual fire that burns without fuel.

One option is to spend our lives ignoring the reality of life, like monkeys spellbound by the rattle-drum. We can focus on meaningless activities that keep us busy, help us pass the time, and prevent us from getting bored or distract us from introspecting and reflecting on life.

The other option is to introspect and reflect on life. We can ask ourselves what shapes our decisions and where does our self-

Miniature of Shiva with five heads

image come from. Why are we in certain situations like the petrified deer, and in other situations like the dominant lion? We will realise that notions such as victim and villain and hero are all imaginary constructions, stories within our heads and stories that we receive from society. In other words, they are maya, constructions to fortify ourselves from fear, subjective realities that make us feel powerful.

Maya gives us meaning to survive this world until Shiva, the destroyer, gives us the strength to outgrow fear and hence outgrow dependence on constructed realities. Shiva helps us realise that heroes, villains and victims are creations of fear. When fear is destroyed, there is no hero or villain or victim. Shiva, the destroyer, thus offers wisdom to outgrow fear. This is liberation. This is moksha.

Acknowledgements

I would like to thank all those who helped in the making of the book including:

- R.N. Singh and Dharmendra Rao of Ramsons Kalapratishtana, Mysore for their unwavering support. Most of the handicraft images in this book were provided by them.
- Harsha Dehejia for helping me find the image of Shiva playing dice.
- Swapnil Sakpal, for helping with the artwork.
- For photograph of Kartikeya temple in Pahowa, Kurukshetra, Haryana — Vishal Berwar and Sanjog Gupta.